ALONE IN THE CROWD

Dr Samir Parikh is an eminent psychiatrist working in the field of mental health over the past two decades. He is the director of the Department of Mental Health and Behavioural Sciences at Fortis Healthcare. Under his guidance and leadership, the department works to provide comprehensive mental health services and also conducts specialized programmes for the community. He has been a speaker at various national and international forums on mental health issues. Dr Parikh has conducted various studies which have been published in the media and have helped the community get an insight into mental health issues. Dr Parikh also has a very prominent presence in the media; he has played a key role in enhancing the image of mental health in the country and his views are widely appreciated by people. He is amongst the most well-known experts in the country on mental health issues.
Twitter: @dr_samirparikh

Kamna Chhibber is a clinical psychologist and has completed her M.Phil in Clinical Psychology. She is currently the head, Mental Health, Department of Mental Health and Behavioural Sciences at Fortis Healthcare. She works within an eclectic frame for the treatment of clinical and other related problems in children, adolescents and adults. She has been instrumental in the development and shaping of the Fortis School Mental Health Program. She has been working extensively with schools as well as within the community to promote mental health for over more than a decade. Through her blogs and interactions with media, she has been working towards making mental health a priority for all.
Twitter: @kamna_chhibber

Also by the same authors

Let Him Not Sink – The First Steps to Mental Health: A Manual for Adults Who Work With Children and Adolescents

Raising Confident Children: A 52-Week Guide

Laugh & Learn with Dr Parikh: Study and Exam Skills

Don't Worry: Here's How You Can Keep Your Mind Fit During a Pandemic

How to Engage with Your Kid While Working From Home: 21 Tips for 21 Days

ALONE IN THE CROWD

OVERCOMING LONELINESS OF URBAN LIVING

SAMIR PARIKH & KAMNA CHHIBBER

RUPA

Published by
Rupa Publications India Pvt. Ltd 2021
7/16, Ansari Road, Daryaganj
New Delhi 110002

Sales centres:
Bengaluru Chennai
Hyderabad Jaipur Kathmandu
Kolkata Mumbai Prayagraj

Copyright © Samir Parikh and Kamna Chhibber, 2021

The views and opinions expressed in this book are
the authors' own and the facts are as reported by them
which have been verified to the extent possible,
and the publishers are not in any way liable for the same.

All rights reserved.
No part of this publication may be reproduced, transmitted,
or stored in a retrieval system, in any form or by any means,
electronic, mechanical, photocopying, recording or otherwise,
without the prior permission of the publisher.

P-ISBN: 978-93-5520-125-6
E-ISBN: 978-93-5520-132-4

Second impression 2024

10 9 8 7 6 5 4 3 2

The moral right of the author's has been asserted.

Printed in India

This book is sold subject to the condition that it shall not,
by way of trade or otherwise, be lent, resold, hired out, or otherwise
circulated, without the publisher's prior consent, in any form of binding
or cover other than that in which it is published.

Key Contributors

Divya Jain
Mimansa Singh Tanwar
Nishtha Narula
Tanushree Sangma

Contents

Message from Dr Samir Parikh — ix

Section I: There Is a Problem! — 1

1. The Changing Landscape of Relationships — 9
2. Shackled to the Desk — 18
3. Rising Cost of Living — 27
4. The Desire for More — 36
5. Everyone Wants a Piece of Me — 45
6. The Devil Called Competition — 53
7. The Noise and the Traffic — 61
8. Sleep Is Missing — 70
9. Cravings Emerging — 79
10. Gadget-o-mania — 89
11. The Evasive Outdoors — 98

Section II: Take Stock — 105

12. Acknowledge the Problem — 112
13. Knowing Is the First Step — 120
14. Building Psychological Flexibility — 129
15. Bring in Work-Life Balance — 136

16. Indulge and Prioritize Yourself	144
17. Look for Solutions	152
18. Hold Your Feelings in Balance	160
19. Invest in Relationships	168
20. Digital Detox	175
21. Focus on Lifestyle	183

Section III: Mindful Urban Living	191
Section IV: Adapting to Change: Learning from the Pandemic	203

MESSAGE FROM DR SAMIR PARIKH

Urban loneliness has been a rising concern over the years. The COVID-19 pandemic has further highlighted the need to direct more attention towards this aspect. There is a substantive necessity to consider ways and methods to combat this problem of urban loneliness, which is setting into the minds of people, particularly the youth. A reflective, introspective approach is required to bring about a shift in the mindset and the approach to tackle it.

While not every individual who is experiencing loneliness will develop a mental health-related illness, the reality is that it will certainly affect people's mental health and state of well-being, which could be detrimental to levels of happiness, satisfaction, the relationships they have and their productivity at work and in their homes.

Through the course of this book, we have outlined the ways in which loneliness has pervasively become a part of urban living and the insidious manner in which it affects many. Often-ignored aspects of the spaces we occupy and the life we live are highlighted to create an awareness of what is and has been going on. Concurrently, we share ways in which this can be effectively tackled both at individual and societal levels and highlight the need to engage in more mindful ways with our own lives. There are several learnings we have derived from this pandemic which have highlighted the need to adapt and bring about sweeping changes in how we do things.

This book is a step in the direction of enabling individuals to develop an approach that would make them more connected to themselves, the people around them and the environment they are occupying.

Section I

There Is a Problem!

problem: A question raised for inquiry, consideration or solution
A source of perplexity, distress or vexation
An intricate unsettled question

The dynamicity of our lives has led to an upsurge in the problems of urban existence. Complexities arise out of this inherent multidimensionality, often creating conflicts and loneliness. Time has become a commodity that is largely missing and highly valuable. 'Busy' is the most common and prominent adjective characterizing the way we live life.

Pick a conversation and you'll find evidence attesting to how busy everyone's life is. Take the example of the following situation:

> You dial a friend's number; it rings a few times and you hear a pre-recorded message stating, 'The number you are calling is currently busy. Please try again later.' Your friend disconnects the call. You assume she's busy—must be at work or doing some important task. When you do manage to get through and finally have a conversation, you hear your friend say at the other end of the line, 'Hey so sorry...I'm busy this weekend. Got so much to do. Work has been so

horrible these last few weeks and I have a lot of home stuff that I need to wrap up. Can't manage this weekend at all. Take a rain check?'

You are left with the craving to connect with someone who you can have easy conversations with, someone who values you and whose insights you cherish. 'Busy' is the most prominent adjective in our dictionaries; in fact, we have created a culture where being busy is a valued attribute. If you are not busy, it may be inferred that there is something wrong with you and how you lead your life. Your ability to be relaxed and take it easy can be perplexing and your easy availability can be an indication of lack of occupation. You may be characterized as the quintessential *vella* (as is used colloquially in the Hindi language to indicate someone who is free and often up to no good)—a reference that you, most certainly, will not appreciate. So you strive hard to stay away from being characterized thus.

It is also possible that you think, 'How is it that I am always free and trying to make plans?' This question can be vexing and a source of distress. In our work as mental health professionals, we encounter this question numerous times, as our clients raise it, sometimes to themselves and sometimes to us, wondering aloud: 'Am I doing something wrong? Should I not be busy too?'

Your Busy Life

In running away from being free, you are tempted to take on far more than what you may ideally want to. It is often the case that the pile of items on your to-do list becomes a never-ending scroll. You, perhaps, often find yourself moving from one item to the next, barely getting a chance to catch your breath, hoping to finish all that's listed so you can find the time to relax and take a breather. But this is likely to be a continuous and vicious cycle.

You, simultaneously, find it impossible to leave things unfinished or simply let them be for the time being. It is also tempting to add more to your plate, which is already overflowing, and you just can't stop. Or, perhaps, will not? And if you are on the path of 'success', then saying 'no' is most certainly not an option. After all, you don't want to jinx your progress and break the streak of 'good stuff' you have going for you.

The paradox is that you do need to slow down, take a break, and perhaps even stop for a bit. But you know you can't get off the bandwagon. In this fast-paced world, with things changing every second, you don't want to miss your chance. What if you slowed down and that's when the opportunity you needed to make it big turned up and you missed it? What if the next person took that opportunity instead and superseded you? What if you will now never get that opportunity again? The 'what ifs' can become burdensome and overwhelming, forbidding the process of slowing down that is so necessary for you to catch a break.

The additional reality is that the busyness of our routines in itself has changed us. It has changed how we think and how our minds respond to situations. We see opportunities and motives in most scenarios. We struggle to keep things simple or to take them at face value. We constantly strive to determine what more can be done. We have a burning desire to achieve more and to utilize every opportunity to ensure success. And to many minds, success appears to be an elusive entity, constantly changing its form and norms. The goal you set for yourself yesterday is no longer sufficient today. It needs continued revision to stand up to what you think society sees as valuable.

So you keep pushing yourself relentlessly, not willing to let go even one bit. Resisting the temptation to do more is hard—in fact, impossible. However, you also realize intermittently that you may be reaching a breaking point. The exhaustion is building up. You can feel yourself snapping and everything within your body wants to stop. There are days when your mind refuses to budge and it's like the ignition of your old car that just refuses to start.

This cyclical contradictory inner dialogue is challenging and disruptive to the tasks you need to do. It creates internal conflict which is difficult to evade. After all, how do you manage to do all that you need to while being pulled in two opposing directions? All along you have learnt to trust yourself—your thoughts and feelings. You repeatedly ask yourself questions like, 'What do I do now?' or, 'Am I setting myself up for failure?'

Maybe what you are setting yourself up for is a *breakdown*. You know you can collapse and what you need to do is slow down. But in the midst of all of this, as you attempt to slow down, you also feel the pangs of being lonely, not having enough people around you to turn to, share and discuss, and seek comfort in.

Lonely in Your Populous City

As the need for 'more' has permeated the psyche of people in urban society, insatiable appetites for material objects, money, power, and to be better than the best, are increasingly preoccupying many. It has led to a situation where more often than not, people experience loneliness.

As mental health professionals, we have constant interface with peoples' lived experiences and the problems they face. We understand the historicity of their lives, delving into the depths of their past and, in doing so, develop a narrative about the roots of their selves and families. Each of us clearly recounts instances where individuals reminisce about their past relationships—the good times with friends and families that have faded away over the years. The sharing of stories is accompanied by a deep sense of loss, of wonderment, if it is for the better or worse.

We, as a society, collectively reflect upon the lonesomeness of our existences. Many describe the feeling of being lonely even when they are surrounded by people. As they live in a city surrounded by millions and yet feel lonely, the depth of the problem cannot be ignored. Others talk of the real deficit of relationships they can turn to in order to seek conversations, nurturance or support. They see people but can't reach them or connect with them. Many reflect on how they foresee a future in which they live alone in eldercare spaces or supported by help. Yet others have glimpses of a time to come when their children would be pursuing their own dreams, their friends occupied in their own individual spaces, their network of family members drifted away and they themselves left alone to manage themselves.

This loneliness becomes anxiety. It creates a constant state of worry, operating almost subliminally, shaping many of our reactions and responses. The mere presence and proximity of others does nothing to make one feel comfortable.

No doubt there is a problem. It is not just an unsolved, unsettling, difficult-to-grasp question. The problem is perplexing and it is an increasing source of distress. It needs consideration. It needs to be understood. A solution must be found. We need to work towards finding an anchor that can more effectively support the existence of many in the urban spaces we have created over time.

1
THE CHANGING LANDSCAPE OF RELATIONSHIPS

Life doesn't make any sense without interdependence. We need each other, and the sooner we learn that, the better for us all.

—Erik H. Erikson

There are times in every friendship when you or your friend are too busy to call or are more focused on other relationships. It will hurt, but it's rarely personal.

—Rachel Simmons

We invest less in our friendships and expect more of friends than any other relationship. We spend days working out where to book for a romantic dinner, weeks wondering how to celebrate a partner or a parent's birthday, and seconds forgetting a friend's important anniversary.

—Mariella Frostrup

In a city high-rise, sitting in the balcony of a twenty-fifth floor apartment and sipping tea, you look out into the horizon, city lights glimmering in the distance, cars fading away as they rush across the highway. You are surrounded by silence though you can hear the faint noises of the horns honking on the roads. You look across at the building angularly adjoining yours and see shadows move across the large expansive windows. You wonder what they could be doing—their conversations, their actions—the scuttling and scurrying movements make you wonder. You can feel the melancholy, the lonesomeness. You reflect on how it was never like this before.

Being Social Beings

Aristotle called human being 'a social animal' and, in many ways, we demonstrate a strong need to belong. Spending time with others, exchanging notes with them, having fun, engaging and stimulating conversations, these are what most people look forward to. Starting from the time you began to speak, perhaps even before that when you could just babble, you have shared experiences beginning with your family members, then with teachers, friends and acquaintances and, later, with your colleagues.

It is your lifelong dependence on others for varying needs that puts relationships at the very centre of existence. As a child, you sought comfort and support in your parents. As a college student, you looked forward to good moments with friends. As a lover, you sought your partner. As a husband or wife, you sought each other for a life together and to have children. As someone who lost a close relationship, you sought it elsewhere, looking for that comfort of familiarity, love and support. As a colleague and co-worker, you sought each other's inputs to keep striving forward and climb the ladder of success.

You have hung on to others through your life to grow and thrive and this has been mutual and reciprocal. These social interactions within the rubric of your relationships have been important and relevant to your existence. They give you purpose and meaning, make you feel alive because you are needed and wanted. As philosopher Benedict de (Baruch) Spinoza observed, 'Men do derive from social life much more convenience than injury.'

Much of what you think, feel and do is a reflection of what has been grasped through the medium of social experiences. Whether these interactions happen within the context of individuals specifically, or the media in general, the influence and impact are enormous. The varying landscape of social interactions and influences shapes the ways in which you see things, come to know them, understand them, define them and even determine what to do with them.

In feeling that you belong, you find your happiness, satisfaction and a sense of well-being. Anyone who has experienced exclusion, isolation or ostracism knows the impact it has on their moods and thoughts, creating anxiety, leaving them feeling hurt and rejected. In fact, we label this aspect as being a form of emotional abuse, which attests to the strong negative impact that such behaviours can have on a person.

Nevertheless, despite the knowledge and an understanding of the need to have and be supported by close relationships with others, we find that these are in a phase of transition.

Relations Are Transactional

A transactional pattern has emerged which characterizes many relationships today. Even within the context of your closest relationships, you may have noticed that there is enormous give and take. Often, if you want someone to do something, you may find yourself negotiating in attempts to strike a deal. Regardless of whether it is your parent, partner, child, friend, employee or colleague, you perhaps find yourself telling them, 'If you do this, I will do that for you' or 'I do this for you all the time, why don't you go ahead and do it for me?' You may have even heard another person say, 'Why should I if they don't?'

By creating this pattern of transactions we have arrived at a world ridden with individual self-interests. People find their motivations to do things if they feel they too are being benefitted in some way through them. The concept of selfless commitment to the welfare of another with whom we share a relationship does not necessarily find much prominence around us on a regular basis. People weigh the relative benefit of their input as against the output they are likely to achieve.

This economical way of engaging with people compromises the connectedness we feel with them, increasing distances in relationships. The genuine consideration for another and regard for their welfare does not appear to be a big driving force for many. It detracts from the satisfaction and contentment we feel in our relationships, making modern-day relationships rather suboptimal in their quality and the kind of backing they provide.

The other facet of this conundrum is that when you are not in a position to reciprocate, you are also reluctant to receive from another. You strive to keep your relationships in a balance, not wanting to be overwhelmed by the commitment, availability and actions demonstrated by another. Something simple like wishing someone or buying a present for them also happens for many if they have received the same previously or they believe their gesture will be reciprocated in the future. If the permutations and combinations result in a potentially low likelihood, then the chances of you wishing and gifting too diminish. Though, of course, if the other person is in a deeply debilitating circumstance and your mind attributes it to an uncontrollable predicament in their life, you are likely to step forward without having expectations of what you will receive in return.

Relations Run on Autopilot

In your busy life, you barely have time to take a breath and assess your own thoughts, feelings and experiences. You typically wake up at a fixed time, go through the same morning routine, rush to and back from varied tasks and responsibilities, get back home at the end of the day and crash after all your chores. You barely register what courses through your body and brain as you manage everything and then you are back in the same cycle the very next day.

As such, you simply can't accord that same time and space to another person. For most modern relationships, the reality is that they run mostly on an autopilot mode. The patterns that have been set over months and years are what get replayed continuously. This is most certainly frustrating, as you continuously get disconnected from each other and feel the resentment grow in your relationships. Even though you may intend to be available for those around you—your family, friends and colleagues—you struggle even to do this for your own self.

The key to strong relationships lies in the attention given to them, caring for them and consciously being attuned to the other person in the dynamic. The time and space to be mindfully engaged to each other is largely amiss. This most certainly compromises the quality of the relationships, reducing our mutual responsiveness to each other. At times when you need to speak with someone, you may find yourself struggling to find that someone.

By the time this aspect gets highlighted, it has usually reached a position where there is a significantly large disconnect that you feel with the people in your life and, pulling back from that, can be rather hard work.

Relations Are Devoid of Real Engagement

Modern-day lifestyle and advancements in technology have led to a continuous replacement of age-old, tested, reliable methods of associating with others. Instead of getting up and going out to meet people and having in-person interactions with them, you are more likely to text them or comment on a post they may have shared on their social media account.

Your understanding of what goes on in their lives is largely derived from what you see on these platforms. Little do you realize that this tends to be a rather incomplete understanding as people are likely to share the evidently good moments of their lives and not speak of their troubles and struggles. As a result, you miss out on a significant portion of what has been happening in their lives, believing that all is well, whereas they may be facing many difficult circumstances.

You perhaps experience the same from those you are connected to. As the range of conversations comes down and texts, calls and status updates come forward to replace them, you find yourself increasingly distanced, disconnected and lonesome in your experiences through your life. Losing that channel of communication, which kept you engaged to each other, results in stress and strain that can characterize your relationships, making you feel lonely though, technically, you have thousands of friends and followers on your social media platforms.

Relationships Need to Bring Excitement

You find yourself driven to find excitement, not just in life but in your relationships as well. Sayings like 'We live one life' have come to characterize the beliefs of many, implying that in living this one life, they need to derive the maximum out of it. What people forget is that the one big aspect that relationships bring is stability. They help in keeping people settled, with their feet firmly planted on the ground. The role of relationships of any nature is to enable the fulfilment of social and emotional needs, helping you grow and aspire towards bigger goals and continually finding meaning and happiness.

In contrast, when you keep moving in search of excitement, you don't realize but you start neglecting those strong relationships of many years. Inadvertently, you keep getting drawn to new people and new experiences. Since you are also very busy, and barely have the time to reflect on what you are doing, the choices you make and their impact occur spontaneously, without you realizing it, till a lot of time has elapsed and much has been altered.

The mindful nurturance your relationships need, the attention you need to divert towards them and the careful scaffolding you need to provide them, if left undone, causes you to lose the strength and support they have always provided.

Relationships Aren't for Me

To assuage the distress that you experience when you fail to connect meaningfully, you perhaps begin to think that relationships are probably just not for you. You spiral in the midst of inner thoughts like, 'You do best on your own. People only complicate things. Let's just stay away from them.' You feed your thought process, sometimes consciously and often times unconsciously, preparing yourself for a life where you will be alone.

Somewhere, you have perhaps adopted a defeatist attitude when it comes to your relationships. You have employed a mechanism that allows you to protect yourself, while still compromising your well-being. Your reaction to the prevailing situations tends to take on an emotional tone instead of trying to find a solution to the problem you are seeing. In doing so, you have created a strong possibility that you will find yourself avoiding people, refraining from immersing yourself in social engagements, finding ways to avoid being in social situations and further isolating yourself.

This pattern tends to compromise your happiness and satisfaction more. Though, initially, it is likely that you will feel better on account of the relief you experience in having taken control of the situation, albeit in a manner contrary to what you would have ideally liked. It, nevertheless, leaves you feeling disturbed and discontented in the long run as it taps into your anxiety and fear of being alone and lonely in this big world, with a good number of years ahead of you.

We Continually Change and Adapt

Change can result in monumental transformations in your life. It can hit you like an avalanche or sneak up on you like a glacier. It can occur in the form of catastrophic tragedy or it may be represented by a broken relationship or a lost friendship. It may result in minor transitions or it may feel like your whole life has shifted. Change doesn't always leave you feeling negative but may, instead, reveal enormous opportunities. The direction these changes take is largely contingent upon the choices you make and, when it comes to relationships, there is much that you can do to alter this shifting landscape.

2

SHACKLED TO THE DESK

Never get so busy making a living that you forget to make a life.

—Dolly Parton

We need to do a better job of putting ourselves higher on our own 'to do' list.

—Michelle Obama

Real freedom lies in wildness, not in civilization.

—Charles Lindbergh

You reach your office, albeit a little later than what you had hoped for, park yourself at the desk and immediately open your laptop to start your day. Taking a deep breath, you ready yourself to focus, tune in and begin working on answering the plethora of emails lying in your inbox. Half an hour into your work, you lift your head and gaze at the surrounding aisles. You stare into the surrounding silence—everyone clicking away at their keyboards incessantly, staring hard at the screens, some of them murmuring softly into their phones talking to clients. Even as you compose your next response, you hear a notification for yet another mail. The noise bounces off everyone around you, appearing as though it was only audible to you. You imperceptibly shake your head and resume your work.

Humans Crave for the Outdoors

Growing up, a lot of time is spent outdoors. As a child, you would have wanted to go to the park, be in the playground, run around with your friends, explore different spaces, get to know more about nature, understand how things work. There was, perhaps, a fascination with all these and many other things. You may have harboured a need to know and understand the world around. You may have been the child who would repeatedly ask their parents, 'Mummy, Daddy, what is this? How does this work? Why is it like this?' You perhaps were also the child who insisted, as soon as the clock struck five o'clock, 'I need to go play with my friends. I don't want to be at home all the time.'

As you grew older, the need to be outdoors would have undergone a transformation. Even if you wanted to step outside to be with your friends or just go to play or for a stroll, you may not have found the time to be able to do so. Slowly and steadily, your going out would have become more about going for classes, sometimes meeting friends, perhaps going to a restaurant or exploring a mall or a market area.

What being outdoors does is to help you form a connectedness with your environment. Ancient philosophers emphasized how being with the natural environments makes us whole, facilitating the development of our spiritual imaginations. Being outdoors provides a space to build social connections, allowing you to engage and interact with people around you and to develop a sense of community and belongingness.

Frederick Law Olmsted, one of the pioneers of urban landscaping, recognized that people need nature to get along with each other, be their best selves, de-stress and relax. He created the famous Central Park in New York with this viewpoint, providing the working classes easy access to a green space.

The Japanese emphasize engaging in *shinrin yoku* or forest bathing that is seen to engage all the senses. Engaging in the natural world allows the employment of all our senses, creating a push for the mind to relax. The fact is, modern spaces and lifestyles emphasize being inside, working and living indoors. This, consequently, limits the utilization of all our senses and most sensory experiences tend to primarily involve the eyes and ears. The fatigue can be high and, the stress experienced on account of being restricted to these closed spaces, is intense.

Productivity Is Key

Every organization looks to optimize its functionality. It seeks large profits and productivity is a key to greater effectiveness in achieving the organizational targets. Being productive translates into utilizing the human resource potential of the organization to the fullest. This implies the need for individuals to understand what they are doing, why they are doing it, how well they are doing it and how they can make changes to do it better. It also means optimally seeking to allocate other resources that are critical to the productivity of the organization.

Somewhere, in all of this, you may feel that the individual gets relegated to the background. It is possible you may develop the feeling that what goes on with the people within the system isn't necessarily a priority. More often than not, employees believe that their worth to the organization is directly proportional to the value they generate in terms of revenue streams and profits. The non-tangible aspects of the roles they play get easily sidelined and remain largely ignored. Even though higher productivity can mean greater economic benefits for the employee, that may not be enough to make them feel happy.

In seeking to improve how individuals work by looking at what supports their efficiency and the outputs they generate, a thought process can get created that leads to assumptions about the need the system has for enhanced productivity. It automatically begins to reflect on higher levels of stress within the organization. There are reports about disconnect and discontent with the roles people have, as well as dissonance between what they are doing and the vision they may have had about their own selves. You too may experience this. And when these feelings take a strong hold on you, the disappointment is enormous and happiness is doomed.

Ergonomics of the Workplace

The ergonomics of the workplace have been an important matter of consideration. Any organization you work for is keen to look at the design of the space that is usually directed towards ensuring that the chances of injury are reduced. The workplace needs to be safe to enhance employee productivity.

More often than not, you will hear questions being asked about how the workplace may be changed so that you can perform better. The idea results from the understanding that a poor workplace design can result in employees feeling fatigued and frustrated, leading to reduced productivity. Concurrently, there is a need to provide more comfortable settings for the employees.

Often, in all of this, the human need to be outdoors is usually forgotten. What results is a workplace that looks great, with wonderful cubicles or workstations that are comfortable and designed for safety, but which is disconnected from the outside. The stark distinction between the inside and the outside of a workplace can be perplexing and often takes away from the happiness you may experience when you are at the workplace.

Health Is Correlated with Safety

Workplaces have a strong commitment to the health of their employees. Over the years, this aspect has gained prominence as organizations communicate to those working in them that the system is strongly committed to their health. You may have discovered across the different places you have worked at or known of that there is a focus on the physical health of an employee. This is often even extended to include the family of the person working within an organization.

Other aspects that relate to health may not always find a significant place. Considering that health usually also includes spiritual and mental health and well-being, these elements often get ignored or given lesser importance than what may be needed within a system. Recent years have begun to see a shift in this respect but, you would agree, much remains to be done in this regard.

Major steps are taken when it comes to looking at and ensuring an employee's safety. However, the same is often not done with regard to happiness. Often people report their workplaces to be their least happy places, frequently on account of the disconnect from the outdoors—a reality that may not get factored into what an organization thinks of when considering employee health and well-being.

Achieving Targets Means Being at the Desk

You know you have targets to achieve. Most work involves delivering a certain output that allows for profitability and growth for both the organization as well as for you. In order to ensure that you are growing within the system, you are likely to push for a little extra work. It may mean spending longer hours, sometimes even working at home, taking on more tasks and going above and beyond what you are committed to do. It's possible that the thought of another colleague moving ahead of you drives you. Or perhaps, what acts as a motivator is the recognition that there are many people who strive to acquire the job you have. You may also be intrinsically driven, wanting to achieve more soon so that you can get your promotions and do well at work.

You need to spend more time sitting at that very desk which you feel tired of. Even if you want to take those breaks, it may be difficult to do so since you know your targets are immovable as is the time needed to finish them. The thought of going off on a coffee break with your colleague is tempting, but it can seem unachievable. You feel you are constantly being monitored, your progress being checked. If you move around too much, your supervisor may start hovering around your desk. You want to avoid any discomfort and conflict so you are likely to stay put at your desk, not moving till you succeed in achieving your target for the day.

Communicating through Gadgets and Apps

Today's generation is inundated with information, thanks to technological advances. Every day, a new gadget and a new platform is devised that changes the landscape of how people communicate with each other. Work is no different in this respect. Every organization wants to smoothen the process of interactions between people, enhance the speed of information transmission and reduce the possibilities of missing out sharing vital information. New communication tools are brought into play as a regular feature. Often this happens at the cost of in-person direct interactions.

Somehow, the advances hold the potential to lead to a paucity of personal connectedness between people at the workplace. Most communication gets directed through the medium of impersonal means and mechanisms. The general lack of time also takes away from being able to demonstrate an interest in what goes on in another person's life. Conversations mostly revolve around work and what you need to do or how you feel about what you need to do and the people you work with or under. The rest of your life gets relegated to the background as a barely existing reality.

Herbert A. Simon, an American economist and psychologist, stated, 'A wealth of information creates a poverty of attention.' Technology has been able to successfully take away your mindful presence in daily interactions. It has been able to make you less attentive to the minute details of what a person may be thinking or feeling in a situation. While it has provided you the freedom to interact, it has reduced the personal engagement you may have otherwise shared with people and replaced it with more task-oriented interactions.

Life Is Impacted

The whole process of working, putting in longer hours, achieving targets, is often accompanied by taking work home. When you know you have things to do and work to finish, it can be difficult to simply put it aside and draw a firm boundary around the time you spend doing your work. You may even find yourself sitting at home responding to emails, taking work calls, drawing up documents and creating your work product. Most days, you may be happy doing it as it gives you a sense of accomplishment. But then there are days when you feel irritated and frustrated by the manner in which work impinges upon your overall life.

Your friends and family members' complaints keep nagging you at the back of your mind. There are times when you wonder what the purpose of it all is and where would it lead you to. And the days there is a disagreement at work or a situation with your supervisor where they are unhappy with your work results, you can feel the discontent and unhappiness boiling over. Thoughts like, 'What's the point? It's never enough,' course through your mind and create enormous restlessness in you. It makes it difficult to justify the life you have created for yourself.

The trajectory on which you are is seemingly repulsive. Despite the things that you do for yourself—the walks, the books, gym and sporting activities, art and creativity—you still feel discontent and disconnected. Your relationships wither away, not just at work but outside of work as well, in your personal space. Despite the appraisals you receive, happiness is elusive.

Finding the Balance

Balance is the key. We need to balance health, safety and productivity and focus on building an environment that is sensitive to well-being and the social needs of those who work in an organization. A complete transformation alone is not the answer. Small steps, which can lead to big results, can be taken. The willingness and wilfulness to make this transition is the key.

3

RISING COST OF LIVING

There is a high cost for low living.

—Edwin Louis Cole

Don't tell me where your priorities are. Show me where you spend your money and I'll tell you what they are.

—James W. Frick

Problems are the price you pay for progress.

—Branch Rickey

In your living room, sitting in front of your television, you wonder about what you should watch. You browse through the news channels—they were always your favourite. But you have recently found yourself hesitating to watch the news programmes. They make you feel anxious. You feel wary of stories that look at the rising cost of living. You don't want to hear about how things are getting more expensive and the pressure everyone is experiencing. You don't want to know how the economy is doing or how some crops are failing. You don't want to hear about the lack of rains or excessive rains. You don't want to be tormented by thoughts of how everything is contributing to rising costs. You would rather stay oblivious, unaware of what is going on out there. You feel irritated with yourself; after all, you have never been like an ostrich—you had always faced problems head-on.

Everyone Wants Progress

Growth and progress are perhaps our most cherished dreams. Starting from a young age, you would have realized the value of growth. It was probably emphasized in all your interactions when you were at home and in school. Each step you took in your life needed to lead to the accomplishment of some higher, more desirable goal. Each activity was directed towards the attainment of skills. Each interaction was expected to contribute towards the enhancement of knowledge. All that you consumed from the media was supposed to lead to the acquisition of more information.

All in all, a strong emphasis is laid on becoming mature, gaining greater wisdom, becoming an evolved being, so to say. This progress on your personal front, it is assumed, would lead to growth and progress later on as well, when you start a job. Ultimately, it would benefit the whole society as you would continue to be an actively contributing citizen.

Today, you may discover yourself talking about progress and growth in your relationships. You question your association with others, giving considered thought to how they are contributing to your personal growth. You want to build relationships that make you think, question, be creative, give perspective, are challenging and make you feel like you are evolving.

You want growth in the country that you live. You want to see the gross domestic product (GDP) rising and the economy booming. You want to hear of the stock markets soaring and there being ever-increasing opportunities for employment. You want to see the landscape change and transform into a modern kaleidoscope. The continuing transformation of the space you occupy in your city becomes an indicator of the growth and progress, or their lack thereof, in your mind.

Even as you hope and strive towards this growth and progress in every domain of your life—personal, professional and social—you can't run away from the distant realization of the costs that need to be borne to achieve this end.

Progress Often Happens at a Cost

As individuals and society take stride in advancements and progress, each step comes with its own impact in the form of both direct and indirect costs. On the one hand, it leads to an enhanced quality of living, assuming that you are able to afford the price these changes come with. On the other hand, it increases social distance between individuals, creating an ever-increasing gap between those who are able to keep pace with the changes and those who are unable to afford them. An additional factor is the enormous climate and environmental changes that are triggered, impacting the quality of life.

Consider this situation that can be broken down on the basis of some broad factors. There is an increase in automobile manufacturing because of higher demand. You assume that the rising purchasing power of the populace for cars would be a boon for the economy. What you forget to question is *how* this purchasing power is growing. It's because of the big banks, providing easy loans to their customers. This creates increasing levels of debts, indirectly affecting people's stress levels, and a pressure to maintain a certain level at which they operate to be able to continue affording these luxuries.

Similarly, the potential impact that the higher demand for cars, which led to rising productivity, has on the environment was overlooked and today you face a situation where traffic jams and increased levels of pollution are a real health hazard. So, inadvertently, you spend more time travelling on the roads, burn more fuel (a depleting resource which we are trying to find alternatives for) and try to find measures to take care of your health. You may be going to more doctors due to respiratory concerns and spending more on purchasing all the fancy gadgets that purify the air. All the while, of course, you cannot forget the detrimental impact it is having on your quality of life, which is compromised because you can't perhaps step out as much, meet friends or socialize the way you used to.

In being preoccupied with attempting to grow, develop and progress, we can find ourselves potentially slipping up when it comes to determining the real impact and cost of it all. The fact is that, every step taken contributes to the rising cost of living and we often don't realize it.

Stress Rises with Rising Costs

Rising costs undoubtedly cause stress levels to soar. You may feel like you are the circus tightrope walker, perilously close to the edge, as you work your way through the labyrinth of everything you need to do to improve things and see progress happen. You make numerous decisions and choices during the course of your day and these can make you experience a rise in your stress level. You assume that it's hardly a possibility but you surprise yourself every time this happens. This feeling gets compounded as you feel the pressure to better the quality of life you are leading.

There is a continual need to think, plan, strategize and make decisions. Improving standards of living and having more facilities do come at a cost. To run a smooth, well-oiled machine at home and your workplace, you can't run away from dipping your fingers in multiple things. You recognize that you would have to do much more in the future to keep things going at the pace that they are currently at. Maintaining the same pace of working or slowing down is unthinkable. That would mean losing the quality of life you are currently used to. So you must keep the pressure on and ensure that you do not succumb to the stress. However, this does not necessarily come with a conscious, deliberate attempt to engage in self-care.

You may experience headaches and body aches or feel exhausted. There may be days when you want everyone around you to quieten down or you may seek a spot where you can run away from all the noise and chaos. There are points in time when you just don't want to get out of bed. Sometimes you may even reflect on how you were perhaps happier when you earned much less. But then, you immediately retract that thought. You know you weren't happy even then. At that time you wanted what you have today. But now it seems that the very things you strove for earlier are hard to retain and maintain.

What bothers you most prominently is the recognition that the means that seem sufficient today, would not be so tomorrow. It is a given that to maintain the life you have, you would need increasing resources. This thought is likely to play repeatedly in your mind. When it is linked to the fact that you may, in fact, have more responsibilities later, it becomes even more burdensome. It can trouble and torment you, not letting you get restful sleep at night.

Many worry about when the next salary will hit their account so that the pressure eases up, albeit only for a few days, till the cycle restarts. You hope and wish for no new random expenses that month at least. If, somehow, you do manage well in one particular month, you find yourself back at the starting line in the next one. So what you do is to dive head first into the deep end of your work despite all the stress that surrounds you.

There Are Burgeoning Expectations

It is a given that as one need is satisfied, another emerges to replace it. There are expectations that line up on all fronts—those that you have of your own self, those that others have of you and those you perceive that others have of you. You experience an increase in stress and pressure on account of these burgeoning expectations.

Concurrently, nobody wants to feel like a failure or be perceived as one either by significant or non-significant others. We grow up hearing questions like, 'What will X say?' or 'What will Y think?' This is easily internalized in your psyche and you often find yourself being sensitive to the perceptions of what others must be thinking, feeling or stating. It isn't just related to what they are actually saying or doing, rather it's *your* thoughts on what they may be saying or thinking. You don't want to feel like a failure and it wrenches your heart at the thought of letting your loved ones down by not meeting their expectations.

All these possibilities can create immense pressure and impact on how you interact with others. You can be easily disturbed, distressed or angered, especially when the stress levels are high. It may feel like things can potentially crumble even as you feel completely drained and exhausted.

The tussle to stay on top of things is difficult. Slipping back and having to operate in a space that is deficient in comparison to what you currently have is an absolutely dreadful thought. After all, besides the enormous adjustment that it may require, it could also be the source of great embarrassment and strife in your life.

Disconnected and Disengaged

Progress brings with it additional challenges even on the personal front, in the context of your relationships. These are often easily ignored as you find yourself taking their existence for granted. But they can and do become a great source of distress, especially if they keep getting relegated to the background often. It's a paradox that as you rise up the ladder, meet others' and your own expectations, people may still remain disappointed with you as they may feel you are being increasingly distant, less involved and attuned to what is going on with them. Your relationships can, thus, experience stress and strain as a by-product of the life you lead.

As you do more and more to afford the lifestyle you have, you keep stepping away from the things and the people you love. You can find yourself in situations where you may need to compromise on something pertaining to your relationships in order to ensure that nothing impacts the work you do and the livelihood you earn. You may find yourself making these difficult choices despite your inherent knowledge that it may result in increasing the distance from your loved ones, leading to more disconnect from them.

Even as you move through these situations, vaguely and at times more acutely aware of the possibility of troubles emerging in your relationships, you can't afford to step away or step down from the roles you need to fulfil. So you find yourself pushing forth to continue in the same direction. It isn't as if you will make absolutely no efforts to redeem your relationships. But it is possible that the repetitive occurrence of such scenarios becomes overwhelming for others as they struggle to justify them and force themselves to let go of what they feel are repeatedly missing or wrong in the relationship.

We Can Take Stock

Assessing and evaluating occur spontaneously, subliminally, at times without conscious awareness and at other times with greatly considered thoughtfulness. These processes that occur are skills you develop and nurture. You learn to understand the mechanisms through which you need to make choices by determining the variables you must consider when making your assessment, and evaluating the potential options you see in front of you. Your ability to take stock and engage in these processes of assessing and evaluating will lead you to make choices that are truly beneficial for you—not just in terms of the economics of the life you live but the other intangibles—including your interests, hobbies, relationships and goals. Creating foresight, through the processes of reflection and introspection to identify the areas of future change, is most certainly a possibility that must be explored.

4

THE DESIRE FOR MORE

A wise man will desire no more than what he may get justly, use soberly, distribute cheerfully, and leave contently.

—Benjamin Franklin

To be content doesn't mean you don't desire more, it means you're thankful for what you have and patient for what's to come.

—Tony Gaskins

Success is not in what you have but who you are.

—Bo Bennett

Walking through the shopping mall you peer at your reflection in the glass, wistfully gazing at all the beautiful products in the display window. You see the dreaminess in your expression and then sigh in exasperation. You have been hoping to reach that stage of life for a few years now, where you don't have to keep looking to check whether you have crossed your budget for that month or not. Every time you feel you have moved closer to that stage, you find that nothing much has changed and you are still struggling to accomplish what you feel are the basic requirements for your life. As you reflect, you realize that each month you work exceptionally hard and each year you get a good appraisal. Despite this, each year you struggle to feel fulfilled. A number of things remains unaffordable, outside your grasp. There is a part of your brain which wants to revolt against the perceived unfairness of it all—so much hard work and yet so many desires remain unfulfilled.

Dil Maange More (The heart wants more)

The philosopher Epictetus stated, 'Wealth consists not in having great possessions, but in having few wants.' Over the years, generations after generations have most evidently veered away from this wisdom. We have taken a route which has led us to want more and seek gratification through fulfilling the ever-increasing number of needs. This need has gained popularity across various media and slogans like *'Dil maange more'* have garnered popularity.

In no way have our desires reduced. In fact, you may catch yourself thinking and saying out loud: 'There is scope for more'. Be it growth in a personal or professional capacity, the financial means to purchase goods, the ability to direct your life or the manner in which you live it—you perhaps find yourself seeking more. Your goals constantly evolve and more often than not, with each passing year, they assume larger proportions. This forces you to push yourself relentlessly to stay steadfastly dedicated to the process of building your resources. It inadvertently translates into spending more time at work to ensure you are growing and your capacity to achieve more and buy more is increasing.

In fact, this process would have started much earlier than what you had imagined. It perhaps began when you were a young child who saw other children—siblings or peers—being a certain way and you too were encouraged to be that way. It got strengthened when you entered school and then college and you were reminded how you needed to be the best of the best, beating not just others but also your own self each subsequent year. The idea of 'the world kneels at the feet of those who do well' got implanted in your young mind and thereafter, you strove to ensure that you did not get left behind in any facet of your life as an adult—your work, relationships, hobbies—everything, perhaps, becoming a competitive space in the process.

The Commodification of Life

At the bottom of it all is the increasing commodification of life. Most things are looked at from the perspective of what economic value they hold. Goods, ideas, services, people are all being looked at as mere commodities, in many ways directed towards increasing their output. Many decisions made by individuals and organizations are based on who will or what will lead to the most substantial economic gain. Society is organizing itself around notions of what is the best way to live that will lead to maximum gain.

What this leads to is an alteration of the relationships that were previously untainted by commerce. Things which did not have an economic value associated with them previously are increasingly being seen in light of such factors. It adds the dimension of utility to both objects and people, where judgments of what one does or how one does things are based upon an assessment of their utilitarian value. This further takes away from the natural associations that existed before such commodification permeated the very depths of society. It has wide-ranging implications for the social, political, economic and cultural lives of individuals.

Need for Instant Gratification

Contributing to the trickiness of the scenario of wanting and desiring more is this strong need for instant gratification that has found its way into everyone's thinking. Patience was a virtue extolled by your elders. You were continually reminded of the need to be patient, that you would get what you wanted when the right time came or when the right opportunity presented itself. You were informed about the need to build upon your levels of patience when you were growing up. This was to aid you in living the best kind of life.

The current environment, when most things are a click away, verily takes us away from this virtue of patience. We find instant gratification stealthily creeping into the nooks and crannies of how you operate in your life. You think of purchasing shoes, a rack for your kitchen, an appliance for your house, some furniture for your office and all you need to do is to log on to one of the innumerable platforms available and click on a button. You no longer need to find the time to make that long trip to that faraway store. The natural deterrent to your impulsive shopping no longer exists.

Everything is easily available and there are choices beyond your imagination. What's best is that everything is also returnable. So any hesitation you might have had originally at the back of your mind about whether something would be appropriate or of the quality gets thrown out of the window in an instant. You don't even need to give it a second thought or discuss it with anyone. After all, you do have a substantial period of time available to test out your purchase and even return it if it does not meet your requirement.

Purchasing Has Been Simplified

Today most products are a click away and so is your ability to purchase them. Even if you do not have a big bank balance or you just ran through most of your salary and need to wait for the next one to hit your account, you don't need to wait for that all too tempting purchase. All you need is a credit card with a decent credit limit so you can buy what you want and pay for it later. All your impulses can be easily gratified by this simple transaction readily available at your fingertips.

So in reality, you no longer take time to process and think about whether you really need a particular product or not. The handy credit card comes to your rescue and then there is the corresponding availability of easy EMIs. In the midst of such immense temptation, stepping back and holding off on that purchase seems silly and easily ignorable.

Your mind doesn't necessarily calculate the true costs of what all you are picking up and it does not consider the long-term implications of these choices you are making. In these tempting moments, you easily forget the stress you experience when your account runs on low balance or when you have a hefty amount to pay for your credit card at the end of the monthly cycle. Even as you stick to the minimum payments that are due on your card you know that you are paying heavily in interests, but the idea of restricting yourself is insufferable.

Making all these purchases and living this grand life somewhere also justifies that distance which has crept into your relationships with friends and family. You tell yourself that working more was for the purpose of a better quality of life and if this is what it means, so be it. You don't want to restrict yourself perhaps because you don't want to face the question, 'What am I working this hard for?' At least when you have the possessions, there is a meaning that gets attached to all that you are doing.

Comparisons Are Rampant

Permeating this desire to own and possess more is the complementary knowledge of what another person has. Comparisons are drawn consciously and, many a time, without being aware of the differences that exist in the familial, economic, occupational, social and even spiritual spheres of your life when contrasted with others presumably close to you. You often reflect on what you are doing, how you are doing it, the means you have available at your disposal, the environment you are operating in and how it all differs from that of another.

You are perhaps aware of a feeling of wanting more or even being driven to do more because there are others surrounding you who have now become your benchmark. They don't always occupy this space. In fact, people enter and exit this position in your mind depending on how you perceive them. As you get to where they are today, they get removed from your mind only to be replaced with another. You presume you would be happier and content if only you could keep accomplishing and reaching the level of another. You don't fathom that your internal satisfaction is compromised on account of this constant comparative game.

Even if you are not the one making these comparisons, you perhaps have a friend, a colleague, a family member or a partner who keeps pointing out these differences to you. If you look back, you can recollect the many moments when your parents brought up the accomplishments of a neighbour's child or when your teachers compared your performance to that of a peer. Your boss too, quite often, utilizes the example of a colleague and how well they are doing with the assigned tasks. And then your own mind keeps comparing where you are in life and where others have reached. These others—your friends—are at a stage where they have a happy family and work life, but you don't have someone to return home to. Maybe you don't have a relationship even though you are doing exponentially better at work. It irks you and makes you feel rather restless. It keeps reinforcing that things are missing in your life. You may not be able to share with others this maze of thoughts that impacts you. You feel lonesome even when there are other people around you.

Social Media Reflects the Reality

The social media messages that get filtered and displayed on your account leave you experiencing gaps in your life to an even larger extent. It's like your social media feed knows that you struggle with what others have and it finds ways of showing you those very things that increase your discomfort. Is it reading your mind? Does it know that even though it bothers you, you can't stop looking at them? Your voyeuristic need to know what's going on in the lives of others, to be informed and feel intimately involved in their lives, perhaps, keeps you hooked. You find it hard to stop viewing these feeds even as they keep troubling you.

The more you see the lives of others who you compare yourself with, the more convinced you become of the splendid existence they have. Your mind doesn't realize that it possesses only one vantage point. To have a full view of what others' lives are, other key information is missing. It keeps weaving fabulous stories and building brilliant narratives of what their life is like. You find it difficult to grasp that there is far more to what goes on with others than what their social media platforms display.

You keep sidestepping your knowledge of how most people are reluctant to share what's not going well in their lives. We belong to a society that reinforces keeping problems hidden and shrouded, steering away from letting people around us know what may be going wrong with our life or relationships. It promotes an isolation of challenges you face—your problems are your own and not anyone else's to solve. Yet, you forget that this may be true for others too.

You stay steadfast in your belief about the splendid life they lead and keep withdrawing into your own shell, consumed by your own thoughts, troubled by your own feelings and restricted by your own actions.

We Can Find Another Vantage Point

Shifting perspectives can be tough. It can make you question how you perceive and think about things. It can hit you like a tornado, leaving much devastation in its path as you struggle to accommodate and assimilate new information. Yet, it creates the opportunity to review and rebuild what you have. Your strength lies in your ability to be adaptable. In pushing yourself to have alternate perspectives and finding other vantage points, you can give yourself the chance to recover much of what you think is missing or lost. You may discover information that can be challenging and yet it allows you to be more relaxed about how your life is moving forward.

5

EVERYONE WANTS A PIECE OF ME

A deep sense of love and belonging is an irreducible need of all people. We are biologically, cognitively, physically and spiritually wired to love, to be loved and to belong.

—Brene Brown

The less I needed, the better I felt.

—Charles Bukowski

We think too much and feel too little. More than machinery, we need humanity. More than cleverness, we need kindness and gentleness.

—Charlie Chaplin

Staring out of the window of a coffee shop early on a Sunday morning, sipping on your cup of cappuccino, you take a deep breath, revelling in the peace and quiet that surround you. You look forward to this weekly Sunday ritual. You call it your 'me time'. Stepping away from everyone, leaving behind all thoughts of your tasks and targets, you engage in this weekly habit to cleanse yourself of all the demands that get placed on you daily. You need the breather as you often get the feeling that you want to break free. You hate it when the feeling resurfaces that everyone wants a piece of you—everyone wants what they need and have their own expectations. And like a ping-pong ball, the question, 'What about my needs?' reverberates in the recesses of your mind.

Human Beings Have Needs

Being human, in its essence, involves having needs. These needs range across the numerous varying domains of life and are integral to its continuity. You may contemplate about the objectives and origins of human actions and, in order to find the answers, you would need to turn to an understanding of human needs. When American psychologist Abraham Maslow first spoke of human needs in 1943, he looked at it in a hierarchical format. He identified that the basic needs range from those that are integral to daily existence requiring the provision of air, food, shelter, sleep and sex, to name a few. But he understood that people are not purely motivated by these basic needs. The acquisition and satisfaction of this level of needs would lead to the emergence of ones at the next level, which are more complex.

The satisfaction of the basic physiological needs leads to the emergence of the need for safety and security. This need is satisfied through the availability of resources, people to help, the presence of moral and ethical codes of conduct, availability of employment as well as housing. When individuals view their life as satisfactory in the context of these next level of needs, they see themselves striving to satisfy their need for love and belongingness. They seek friendships and relationships. They actively want to connect with people around them. They want to be acknowledged and loved.

The presence of loving relationships allows a person to consider moving up the ladder towards the domain of esteem needs, which look at elements like confidence, self-esteem and respect from others. Their satisfaction leads to the emergence of cognitive needs, which drive individuals to gain knowledge and understanding, to be curious and exploratory and to find meaning and predictability. Aesthetic needs find prominence as these other needs get satisfied and people seek appreciation and search for beauty, balance, form, etc. Needs of the highest order include the need for self-actualization, which involves realizing one's own true potential, finding fulfilment and the need for transcendence in which a person is motivated by values that go beyond the individual's personal self.

At each stage of life, faced with differing situations, needs continually remain a central feature and driving action, motivating people to do more and do better.

Conflict Arises between Needs, Duties and Responsibilities

Each person has needs that are unique to their individual self. Navigating the path between what you need and what someone close to you may need can reveal challenges. You may find yourself struggling to strike a balance between what your need is and what you see as your duties and responsibilities. It can feel like you are being tugged in two different directions, creating turmoil within you. Each could be mutually attractive or one may draw you in while the other may trouble you, yet both could be equally important.

Take for instance a situation in which you just want to be in your room, reclining in your easy chair, reading a book. But you are aware that your child is in the next room, prepping for an exam. Sooner or later, you will hear her wanting you to help or do a mock test. Each activity is equally important to you and you want to do both. Yet, you feel the internal conflict building up. It's not like you have too much of an option. But you desperately wish for one. What choice do you make? Or is it more appropriate to ask, 'What choice *should* you make?'

Most people find themselves at such crossroads at multiple points during the course of a single day. There are times when the choice is an easy one. And then there are situations which really test you. Constantly finding yourself between the throes of these conflicting thoughts and feelings can be strenuous, increasing the pressure and stress you feel. It can lead to doubts and sometimes leave you feeling disappointed and unhappy. The worst is when you start questioning the purpose of working so hard and not being able to enjoy the fruits of that effort. The dilemmas that arise and follow you like your shadow compromise your contentment with life and the direction it is moving in.

My Needs Don't Take Precedence

The irony is that despite having your own needs, which can be rather strong, you may often pander to the needs of others.

You end up placing their needs above yours or succumbing to what you see as your duties, quashing your own needs to take care of another's. More often than not, these tend to be spontaneous choices that you have internalized over the years across your socialization experiences. Growing up, you saw your parents make choices, you saw family members, siblings and friends make choices, you heard of the choices your role models made and you saw these reflected in the media you consumed. You derived your own notions of what you can do for yourself and the situations where you can push forward your own agenda. What you didn't account for was the feeling that you lived a fairly unsatisfactory life.

You seek someone who would do for you what you perceive you do for others. You constantly stay on the lookout for someone who can prioritize you and what you need. You hope and wish that there will be a situation where what someone else needs is not a priority. Many small and big instances are etched in your mind where you felt you had to give in—the number of times you went for lunch with your friend, the movie you gave up so your partner could watch a match, the show you skipped so your mum could watch what she liked—the list is endless.

You are constantly drawn to ask: 'When will I be a priority?' 'When will importance be given to what I want to do?' 'Am I always going to be the one prioritizing others?' You can feel the constriction in your throat, the catch in your voice and the disappointment in your mind as you wait for someone to think of you and what you need. You keep withdrawing into a shell, hoping for a miracle—a moment when someone, anyone, would let your needs take precedence. In this labyrinth of your thoughts and feelings, you find yourself all alone—waiting to be found by another.

Choice Is a Paradox

As you attempt to illustrate to others how your needs are not prioritized or met, you may hear it being said that these are choices *you* are making. Is that really true? Others around you may feel so and you hope that it is the case. But the reality you face every day reinforces that you don't really have the kind of choice people assume that you do.

There are constraints that you face as you live your life. These tend to be non-negotiable. You are bound to recognize that despite all the emphasis on how you will decide and you will choose, you really don't end up making as many choices. The circumstances of your life, the people who are around you and each decision you have made continually keep restricting the choices you really do have. You may feel like having a sandwich but your choice gets restricted because there is no bread in your refrigerator. You are left with the option of a salad or some cereal. Neither entices you and yet, you now need to decide between the two alternatives in front of you.

Such scenarios are bound to manifest even in the more significant situations of your life. Whether you are at work or at home, there are restrictions that come into play in a fairly automatic way. You may not even realize that these exist because you are so used to their presence. They have become an accepted reality of your life, one that you don't question or even raise an eyebrow at.

Others Around You Are Egocentric

Somewhere in your mind, you may have built the hypothesis that others around you are egocentric. They lack the ability to take on your perspective. What matters most to them relates to their own point of view, regardless of how limited it may be. They lack the empathy to be able to understand where you come from and what affects you. They stay focused on what goes on with their own selves.

You vehemently hold on to the belief that this is how others are. They make decisions based on what works for their own selves. They show limited consideration for what relates to you. You feel left out. You feel unhappy. You feel disconnected from them because your relationship appears to be dependent on what you can do for them and not on mutuality and reciprocity. You feel invisible, as though you don't have a voice or shape in the grand scheme of things.

It has the power to impact your moods, make you feel low, angry, sad, confused, resentful and a host of other feelings, each of which only reinforces how alone you are.

We Can Reclaim Our Spaces

In this ensuing dialogue that makes you feel left out and alone, there is the potential to find your space. You can take steps to enter the field of engagement. You can find ways and measures that allow you to occupy more space within your relationships. You start by determining your needs and follow it up by prioritizing yourself. The steps to do so are many, but recognizing the possibility of this outcome is rather important. Your needs can find their space in this seemingly improbable scenario. What you need to do most is to persist.

6

THE DEVIL CALLED COMPETITION

The ultimate victory in competition is derived from the inner satisfaction of knowing that you have done your best and that you have gotten the most out of what you had to give.

—Howard Cosell

The only competition that matters the most is competing to become better than our best old self.

—Edmond Mbiaka

You can't look at the competition and say you're going to do it better. You have to look at the competition and say you're going to do it differently.

—Steve Jobs

You've just finished your 5-km run and you feel drained, yet exhilarated. You look down at your phone, eager to assess the progress you've been making on your fitness app. Your friend and you have been competing and she has been ahead of you all along. It all started out in a friendly banter, as a medium to motivate each other. Both of you were struggling to stay on top of your fitness routines previously. And so you decided on this challenge. It was supposed to be a friendly one. But now you feel the competitiveness of it seeping in. You don't like it when she is leading and you find yourself constantly trying to beat her.

Everyone Strives to Win

Human beings constantly measure themselves against their peers. Be it a championship at school or in college, a task at work, a bet with a friend or a game with your sibling—in every space, you compare yourself with another. Whatever the challenge you face, you push yourself to find that win. You probably realize that the competition becomes fun as you find success. The lack of a win has the potential to increase your stress. It can make you feel dissatisfied and unhappy. It prompts you to keep finding solutions.

You would have wanted to excel in each task you engaged in. As you grew up, you would have received reinforcement for your successes. Your victories would have been celebrated. Your failures would have prompted rethinking and problem-solving. You would have been encouraged to determine what went wrong. It was perhaps pointed out that you would then be able to know the means to the end of winning.

This competition, along with the strong need to win, finds its space in every aspect of living in society. It is deemed as crucial to survival. It gets automatically linked to your perceptions about your own self. You begin to judge yourself if you don't find enough wins coming your way. You seek them out because they make you feel good about yourself.

They also lead to recognition and appreciation from others around you.

If you are perceived as a winner, you infer it to be a positive reflection upon who you are. It makes you happy to know that people view you as someone who is an achiever, someone who gets to the goals and targets that are set. It keeps your confidence soaring, further contributing to your self-esteem and self-worth.

What you don't realize is that somewhere, you keep shifting the locus of control outside of you. In all this competitiveness and pushing to win, somehow the determinants of your happiness shift outside of you—your happiness and contentment becoming contingent upon prevailing situations and the perceptions of others.

Competitiveness Enters Most Relationships

Competition has been traditionally viewed as a mechanism that allows evaluation and assessment of an individual's skills. It creates the space to make a judgment about who can do what and how well they can do it. It can thus allow for the optimal implementation and utilization of an individual's skill sets. What is forgotten is the inherent nature of this competitiveness which, in an insidious manner, creeps slyly into almost all of your relationships. You may not even realize it and can be faced with a scenario in which most of your relationships are consumed by an underlying competitiveness.

You may find yourself vying to live a life better than your siblings, who you shared the closest bond with. You desire to surpass the level of your peers' achievement. You want meatier projects, more roles, bigger responsibilities and better remuneration than any of your colleagues at work. Subconsciously, you perhaps even find yourself competing with your parents as you strive to provide a comparatively better life for yourself, for them, for your partner or your children.

These competitive strivings influence the very nature of your relationships. They do not allow for the free exchange of ideas, thoughts and feelings so crucial for the creation of strong bonds. Yet, it can be difficult for you to steer away from permitting this process to shape and influence your relationships. So you keep succumbing to these feelings and thoughts; after all, those around you are doing the same. It is a mutual and reciprocal process—not one that you alone are driving or engaging with.

People Won't be Genuinely Happy with My Success

Underlying many people's thinking is the fear, which turns into a belief, that most people around them would not be genuinely happy with their successes. Built on the foundation of thwarted expectations, this feeling can become a strong determiner. When you see the lack of happiness or applause or a congratulatory message from a friend or colleague, your ears prick up. When you notice that your friend turns conversations to herself each time you bring up something that relates to you, you surmise the lack of genuine happiness for you and what you achieve.

These experiences keep influencing what you are thinking about these people around you—your friends, colleagues and family. It impacts the manner in which you interpret their responses and reactions. The evidence you have seen once or a few times may even cause you to jump to numerous conclusions in your mind. You may not fully trust the viewpoints you receive.

Parallel to the positive messages coming your way, you may discover a thought process that reiterates, 'It may not really be how they feel. Beware!' Somewhere behind all the good responses, the shadow of an underlying competitive spirit lurks. It shapes how you feel about peoples' responses. It makes you doubtful of their intent. You may consider them to be fair-weather friends, half expecting them to all disappear at the first appearance of a problematic situation. Or, you may feel that some of them can, in fact, pull the carpet from under your feet and revel in seeing you tumble and fall. Trust can be a difficult virtue to maintain.

One Must Tread Carefully

These notions about how competitiveness enters all relationships, coupled with a lack of belief that others can be genuinely happy for you, creates doubts about how much trust you can place on them. It feeds into ideas about needing to be circumspect in interactions, and taking comments and compliments with a pinch of salt. Often, people are seen to even harbour the thought that the excitement or happiness people demonstrate is just a façade. Internally, they most certainly don't feel this joy and may, in fact, bear feelings of envy or jealousy.

Thinking that your downfall may well be something that

others desire can make you distance yourself from them. You won't recognize it but in your interactions, you may have withdrawn. A distance has seeped into your relationship with the same people you used to share great camaraderie with because you find it counterintuitive that in these times when everyone wants the best for themselves, they can genuinely be happy for you.

So what you do is to further isolate yourself. You restrict what you share, how much you share. It is a reminder of the things you heard elders saying, *'Nazar lag jayegi'* (God protect you from the evil eye). So you want to hide your successes, even when you want them to be known. It's a constant tug of war inside you, qualitatively impacting the relationships you share with your acquaintances to the closest of friends and even family members who you have the fondest memories with.

We Are Averse to the Last Place

Your continuing success makes you averse to failures. It creates anxieties about not being able to reach the pinnacle of success. There are larger fears at the bottom of these anxieties—fears of losing your livelihood, fears of losing your position, fears of losing your relationships, fears of being left alone, etc. All in all, it keeps you averse to being left behind on that last spot.

So, to combat this, you push yourself to keep doing all that is needed to stay away from the bottom of the barrel. Whether you need to do more at work or you need to push yourself in your personal spaces to contribute more to the lives of those you love, you keep doing it without questioning even as you feel the stress rising. You may feel yourself burning out—feeling drained and exhausted, losing your sense of personal accomplishment, feeling disconnected and depersonalized at times from all that's going on around you.

This aversion is like a big pressure bubble waiting to burst at any given point in time. You don't want to be at a spot where you question your capabilities, your goodness or your self-worth. So, it is crucial that you find more ways to manage it. But, what you end up doing is pushing yourself to ensure that you are not in that detested last place!

A Little Competition Is Healthy

It all perhaps starts with the thinking that a little competition has never harmed anyone. Having some amount of competition is rather healthy. Its positivity lies in its ability to act as a motivator, you believe—an external push that allows you to stretch your imagination and flex the muscles of your mind. It lets you know what more can be done. It forces you to develop ways to negotiate with people and situations, and build empathy and tenacity to face obstacles.

You might, nevertheless, miss out on the 'a little' part and get consumed by this competitive spirit across many domains of your life. How you keep it in the 'space of healthy competition' and operate in a manner that it is constructive and not detrimental to your personality and expectations from life can be challenging, testing your patience and wit.

What you may need is to engage in a continuing process of evaluation and assessment of how you are approaching the competition you engage in. You need to work towards not letting it become the sole driving factor in the life you lead, finding more meaningful methods that can become your motivators, shifting the locus of control to your internal self.

We Can Develop an Internal Locus

Though you feel tempted to look outside, seek external validation for a lot of what you think and do, you can shift the locus of control and find your contentment from within you. It is possible to change and become more internal than external—to take personal responsibility for your actions, deal with challenges and stressors better and thrive in the midst of change. People may not change, but you can change what and how much you seek and expect from them.

7

THE NOISE AND THE TRAFFIC

They say the universe is expanding. That should help with the traffic.

—Steven Wright

Never to allow gradually the traffic to smother
With noise and fog, the flowering of the spirit.

—Stephen Spender

The sound of a small bell during a dark night is louder than the din of traffic outside your window during rush hour. Surprise and differentiation have far more impact than noise does.

—Seth Godin

Sitting in your car, you look out of the window, glancing at the car next to you. You see your irritability and restlessness reflected in the faces of those in the next car. Stuck in the slow-moving jam you feel like it's not just your time but your life that is slipping away. It's a feeling you get every day—morning and evening—as you travel back and forth between your home and your place of work. The cacophony of the blaring horns, the blasting music from cars, the vendors crowding the edges of the roads, bikes and cars randomly stopping on the sides blocking the route, cars cutting across each other, all jostling for that extra inch of space they can squeeze their way through—it is all business as usual. And it keeps heightening your levels of annoyance. By the time you get home all you want is some quiet and a bucket-load of peace, a break from all the noise and a breather from this constant need to rush.

The Desire for the Big City Life

When Georg Simmel, the German sociologist, philosopher and critic, chose to analyse the effects of the big city life on the mind of individuals in 1903, even he would not have imagined the relevance it would find in today's world. His words find truth in the manner in which the urban landscape has transformed over the last century and how humans are responding to it. His main contention at the time was that a person living in the city must erect defences and barriers to protect the self from the multitudinous stimuli that they are bombarded with. Look around you and that is the reality today—you face an overstimulating environment that is difficult to keep pace with.

Nevertheless, surrounding you are hordes of people who crave the big city life. They seek the opportunities it can afford them, the lifestyle that they believe follows from the greater economic benefits of residing in it, as well as the availability of enormous resources and options to choose from. In seeking the city life, many people choose to migrate. Most arrive with high expectations, hoping to realize their imagined comforts of existence.

The reality that faces them, more often, is an overcrowded space with unimaginable numbers seeking the same dreams. The pre-existing city dwellers find themselves in a space that is overflowing with people seeking more from a city that struggles to maintain its pace with the changes it needs to undergo to meet the needs and expectations of an exponentially expanding population.

All in all, you find yourself stuck in an environment where many remain dissatisfied and discontent. The struggle is not just to meet the needs and desires that you have. The problem has many more facets to it. You may find questions popping in your mind that make you wonder, 'Even if I get to where I want, is this the way I want to do it? Is the struggle I go through every day a good enough cost to pay for what I seek?'

The things you are losing can, in fact, be far more valuable than you had imagined. It can be hard to acknowledge and accept but the regular, frequent resurgence of such thoughts and questions can be troublesome, making you evaluate your existence and make an attempt to find alternatives, something that can lead to what you want without having to go through the kind of challenges the city life makes you go through. The dissonance can be enormous and troublesome, beyond what you may have ever fathomed, and you may not find someone around you with whom you can share this internal struggle.

Sensory Overload Can Be Depleting

As you move through your day, you absorb an enormous number of stimuli from your environment. Typically, your brain is able to process, manage and make sense of all the stimuli that it receives. However, when it is overstimulated, receiving far more than what it can manage, moving through the day and managing yourself and your tasks can become a problem. It can feel like you are stuck in a room with no doors and no windows, with blaring music, people all around you, everyone talking and making so much noise and you are unable to escape from it all. The presence of any other stimulus, thereafter, would only make things far worse.

It takes away your energy and enthusiasm and keeps leaving you feeling more drained and exhausted. It interferes with your sleep, affects your moods, increases your anxiety, makes you more sensitive to others around you, alters your productivity and diminishes your levels of patience. It makes you want to run away from what goes on around you, prompting you to isolate yourself and be alone.

The very things you crave for—more resources, more people, good relationships and a good life—are the things that can potentially evade you as you struggle with an overstimulating environment. This sensory overload that you experience can be rather debilitating.

Sensory Overstimulation Impacts Health and Well-Being

Study after study has reinforced the fact that being constantly overstimulated can substantially affect an individual's health as well as their mental and emotional well-being. Noise, which is considered loud as per an individual's own unique level of sensitivity, is not the only problem. The presence of background noise too, as a continuous stimulus in the environment, can be rather problematic. This relates more to the noise that an individual does not have control over and not the ones that they consciously choose, such as when a person plays loud music because they enjoy it.

The impact is seen on a person in the form of reduced energy, increased irritability, aggressiveness, low tolerance thresholds, muscle fatigue, muscle tension, hypertension, cardiac concerns, sleeplessness, difficulty in concentration and paying attention to tasks and increased levels of stress, to name a few. The chronic, daily exposure to sources of noise, the presence of which you are keenly aware of, can certainly lead to the exacerbation of such concerns.

Emotional Exhaustion Increases Sensory Sensitivity

The corresponding fact is that if you are someone who feels emotionally drained and exhausted, are fatigued and tired, are feeling more anxious or low, or have too many stressors in your life, these too can increase your sensitivity to sensory stimuli. It is likely that you experience even small noises such as the sound of someone chewing or the clicking mechanisms of doors shutting as big irritants, making you feel as though you are on the edge. You can find your tone becoming sharper, your responses more caustic and your general level of tolerance dipping below what you yourself may consider as being optimal.

Your life may be such that you work to fulfil multiple roles. You may be a student, an employee or a boss at work and parallel to that you also have your personal roles to take care of, that may include being a child, a parent, a partner, a friend or a colleague. The more the roles and responsibilities you hold, the more you can feel stretched, strained and drained. This can become particularly concerning if you also find yourself struggling to maintain your sense of balance.

As you may not have an escape from the things you need to do and the roles you must play, you push and stretch yourself to find that extra bit of energy within you to keep going. It's a relentless vicious cycle because the more you push, the more you feel exhausted, anxious, low or worried; the more you want a break, the lesser its possibility, given the current state of your affairs.

The Surrounding Spaces Are Overcrowded

Occupying the space you do in the city you reside in, you are surrounded by an ever-increasing number of people. The abandonment of rural spaces and increased migration to urban cities, leading to their overcrowding, leads to social, economic, environmental and sociocultural problems as well. The quality of life, regardless of the socioeconomic class you belong to, gets easily compromised. There are issues of substandard housing facilities, poor water supply, sanitation, transport, infrastructure, reduction in availability of good educational and occupational opportunities, as well as environmental degradation.

Overcrowding of the city also contributes to the rising cost of living, besides the poor availability of resources. This overcrowding can be a great source of distress and may challenge you in multiple ways as you struggle to keep yourself calm amidst the rising crowds. You may struggle to walk on the footpaths or find parking in a shopping area. The traffic is certainly a concern but so is the waiting that you need to do if you want to take the metro to a different part of the city. Finding a seat in a public transport, say, a bus can be challenging. And, if you have an emergency, you fail to imagine how you would possibly reach a hospital or a police station on time.

All of this is likely to leave you subliminally worried. You may not reflect on it daily or speak of it regularly. Yet, at the back of your mind, you may find it running about a bit. You may distract yourself from the thoughts but you know they never fully go away. The solutions, you know, are not easy and most of them may feel out of your reach. Yet, you need to find a way to calm down your nerves because this constant worry and anxiousness only serves to make you unhappy, discontent and unable to enjoy what is good around you.

Crowds Don't Create a Feeling of Belonging

Despite the fact that you are surrounded by many people, it doesn't translate into a feeling of belonging. You may have many people who are around you and yet you may not feel a connection with them. The presence of so many people can, in fact, be perceived as threatening and anxiety inducing. This emerges from the possibility that they can usurp the options and opportunities that you can benefit from.

The potential that someone else can take away the benefits you can have, automatically places you in a position of wanting to maintain a safe distance. This is needed so that you don't compromise on and give away the information you have. Your progress and growth are essential to your existence and the interference of any situation or individual is not an acceptable outcome.

So you are likely to build relations which are transactional and not so close that they can harm your progress. At the end of the day, this compromises the possibility of building a close, trusting connection and that certainly does not let you feel like you belong. There is also the chance that you may find a shift in your previouly strong relationships with your siblings, cousins, friends and even co-workers.

We Can Make Difficult Choices

The choices you face are many. A lot of them can be difficult as well. Faced by them, you may feel apprehensive and unsure. You have the option to step forward and move in the direction of growth or step back and do nothing and continue to feel safe. But that may not be the best alternative for you in the long run. As, what perhaps holds more promise is the approach of taking the chance and choosing to do something. It is likely to get you dividends and the life that you desire. Your decisions make you who you are, and doing so will be empowering. It is possible to find the mental energy to not get bogged down by the massive amount of cognitive grit and make the decisions that you need to.

8

SLEEP IS MISSING

And the next morning, when I wake up, I am reborn.

—Mahatma Gandhi

We dream in our waking moments, and walk in our sleep.

—Nathaniel Hawthorne

Insomnia is a glamorous term for thoughts you forgot to have in the day.

—Alain de Botton

Tossing and turning in your bed, you run through all the tasks you have lined up for the next day. You check off the list of things you needed to finish before you lay down in bed. Suddenly, you remember that you forgot to send that really important message. You turn to the other side, forcibly shutting your eyes. You don't want to reach out towards your phone, but sleep evades you. This thought about the message keeps popping up. It isn't letting you sleep. Grudgingly, you toss your sheet aside and swinging out of the bed, grab your phone. You send the text, feeling irritated.

And then your Instagram catches your eye.

One Peaceful Night

Everyone craves for a night when no exigency preoccupies them, no task of the next day runs in their mind, and the evening can be spent doing absolutely nothing—this one peaceful night is mostly an unrealized dream for many. Yet, it occupies a coveted space in the minds of almost all. Imagine yourself on such a day when you get back home from work and there is nothing you need to take care of—no chores to do, no dog to walk, no meal to cook, no cleaning up after yourself, nothing that is pending and nothing that needs to be done first thing the next day. A blissful idea and tempting for sure, but one that you know may not really be realistic or possible.

On most days when you wake up, you find yourself feeling tired even before you have gotten off the mark. The thought of accomplishing your targets for the day and closing all the items that find space in your to-do list, in itself, is definitely exhausting. And as you set off on your day, you absorb an enormous amount of information. Making sense of it all, consolidating it, integrating it and storing it requires tremendous effort—work that consumes a large amount of your energy stores. By the time evening comes, you're tired, and perhaps reminded of your younger years when you would sleep for 12–14 hours, waking up at noon or even later.

Your body doesn't need as much sleep now. You do okay even when you get seven to eight hours. You're not able to stretch your sleep time for much longer even if you really want to—the body just does not switch off for that long. But despite the fact that you need lesser hours to feel the same relaxation and rejuvenation, you don't always get up feeling that great and ready to embark on your journey for the day.

What you do need and do well with is the presence of a consistent sleep pattern. The days when you can maintain your routine are invariably better days for you. Whether you sleep early or late, wake up early or late, you need to implement a certain method to the way you manage your sleep routine. It feels good on the days you have this locked in. And then on the days you're unable to maintain it, you find yourself struggling.

Nevertheless, every day you do think of that good night's rest and a peaceful sleep that would help you feel absolutely fabulous the next day.

Sleep Is Overrated

When you speak to people around you, you realize that many people perceive sleep to be rather overrated. They feel that they could get by with less sleep. They ridicule the assumption that eight hours of solid sleep is necessary for effective functioning. They believe, instead, that sleep is not as much of a necessity. It is not as important as people would have us believe. In fact, they view that sleeping less increases their productivity and makes them feel good.

However, contrary to this belief harboured by many, there is the fact that neither too much nor too less sleep is good for an individual. What you do need is an optimal amount of sleep during the nights. What you also need is for the quality of that sleep to be good. This can only happen when you aren't disturbed by your thoughts, the pending things, the noises from outside, someone snoring or the neighbours playing loud music, the planes flying in the sky or people blaring their horns even as the city sleeps.

It isn't that sleep is overrated. It is just that you need to find the right balance and combination for yourself. You need to gauge what works best for you and then create systems that ensure you are able to achieve it daily as far as possible. Even as you feel tempted to look over your shoulder to glance at what your partner, friend or colleague is doing, you must refrain from doing so.

Late Nights Are the Norm

In the depths of your mind, there is an assumption that if you sleep early, people will equate you with a baby or a child. You don't like to hear of such comparisons. They make you feel like you are viewed as somewhat of a lesser or deficient being. Especially as you grew through your adolescent years, moving through high school and then college, it was reinforced that sleeping early was not becoming of someone that young. You had to be vivacious and full of energy, always charged up to full potential, barely needing any rest or time to relax.

Since those days when you were younger, this notion came to be a part of your identity. All these years you have held on to this belief rather strongly. It's been a way in which your youth defined you and you defined being youthful. So staying up till the wee hours of the night came to be a norm.

It was a given way for you to live your life by, a standard operating procedure of your life.

The impression you've held on to for years has attested to how late nights are the norm—that is what people your age do. Whether you do something substantive or not, are spending time with those you love or not, are doing something meaningful or not, are engaged in some important work or not, what is most relevant is to stay true to what is expected from you.

Besides this idea that was strongly reinforced in your younger years, when you speak to people around you today in your professional circuits, you realize that every individual is doing exactly that. They are spending days staying up till late in the night, not always because they are doing something they love or enjoy, but because that is how things have come to be and one has gotten used to them being this way. So you don't question the late nights; you continue to identify with them and keep pushing yourself to stay true to this part of your identity even if you struggle to grapple with it.

Catching Up with Life Happens in the Night

You look forward to head back home after a long day at work, doing all that you needed to do. You want to get back, have a nice long shower, feel alert and alive, prop your feet up, have some good food and then catch up with life. This process of catching up can be rather long-winded though. It starts with conversations with everyone at home. From hearing stories about their day, to the problems they faced, and narrating the crux of your experiences, a lot of time gets consumed in getting up to speed with each other's lives.

Besides your family, you know you must catch up with your friends. Even though you responded to most of their texts, you may need to return some calls or maybe you still need to get back to those with whom you knew the exchanges would have gone on for longer or which would need more of your attention. And then, there are the social media platforms you need to work your way through. After all, much of what goes on in the world of those you connect with socially is on display there. Missing out on this content is not an option. You would not want to be left behind in the rat race to stay on top and be informed—even if it is about people in your social network.

To do all of this you need time, and time, like we all now know, is a precious commodity. You won't be getting back home early after work. So everything listed above would only come to fruition much later in the evening, or more likely in the later hours of the night. This means to catch up with what is going on in the world around you, sleeping is not going to happen any time soon. And most importantly, whatever your mood may be like, by the time you are done getting up to speed with things, it is likely your sleep is already compromised.

Unwinding = Less Sleep Time

Unwinding is a word that is now more prominently placed in the dictionary of most people. We hear of the tremendous stress people face and everyone who has any input to give about how to manage it is sure to mention the need to be able to unwind. This concept of unwinding is an inescapable necessity. Everyone needs to find a way to recharge and reboot themselves, just the way they do it with their gadgets that get exhausted with continual usage. The human body is no different.

However, this unwinding is contingent upon the time that is available to you. And we can't evade the reality that time is most certainly not available, at least not in the amount that you require. Pushing yourself to stay on top of things non-stop has taken its toll. And if you don't pause to push refresh, then you are likely to lose your edge. That certainly cannot be an option because to meet your goals and reach the pinnacles of success you desire, you need to stay sharp.

So you make adjustments to the time you have available and you do so by stealing some from your sleep. You either stay up till later in the night or you wake up much earlier in the morning. But you try to ensure that you get your daily dose of unwinding that will keep you going through the weeks, months and years. However, you may somewhere feel like you are perpetually sleep deprived. You feel tempted to snatch that infinitesimally small bit of time to get more sleep. But you know that it is not a realistic possibility.

Worrying Makes it Difficult to Sleep

Your sleep is not compromised just because you have so much to do and so little time to do it in, or because you need to catch up with a lot. It is also affected because there is a part of you that stays anxious and alert. As you lie in bed with the lights switched off, you can find your mind wandering over different topics. Even though you may have been feeling extremely sleepy and the day had left you feeling completely drained and tired, sleep can still find its many ways to evade you.

You may ponder over the things that happened during the day, the conversations you had with people and how you could have done them differently, or you may run through numerous thoughts about the past. Maybe you feel preoccupied about what will come up next. There is an underlying anxiousness about future outcomes. You perhaps ruminate about how you would cope if things did not go well or you fantasize about the brilliant possibilities that can happen in your life. You attempt to plan and strategize in your mind on how to live a good life or about how you would find your way through losses and grief. Unknowingly, too much time would have elapsed.

Your worries can become pervasive and persistent. They can be rather unrelenting. They encompass numerous elements and they come and go spontaneously. Every evening you think to yourself, 'Tonight, I must ensure I sleep early. I cannot keep having these late nights followed by such an early start. I'm sure to collapse like this.' Yet, you may find yourself going through the same cycle the next night.

Late at Night the Mind Finds Peace

Going through the chaos of everyday life, there is so much that finds its way to us, prompting us to take action. The days require a continuous process of acknowledging, engaging and responding to multiple people, situations and stimuli. It tends to be a never-ending process from which there is no respite. The only time you find when you are not required to respond and to be at ease is, perhaps, the little time you get at night.

This, then, becomes the one time of the day your mind inadvertently looks forward to. It actively seeks out to find a way to unwind and relax. The lack of any noise, the peace of silence, is an attractive proposition—it draws you in, tempting you to stretch yourself that little bit extra to revel in the tranquillity and peace of night.

We Can Find Many Alternatives

Habituated to our existing patterns, we often feel limited in our choices. We come to believe that what we have been doing is the best alternative. We get restricted in our thinking, stuck to the old ways of being. Yet, if you push yourself enough, you are likely to discover that there are numerous possibilities. Finding these possibilities can be difficult but it is not impossible. You need willingness, openness, flexibility and the will to receive these alternative perspectives.

9

CRAVINGS EMERGING

When eagerness and passion vanish, desire is deserting a weary mind. The power of craving is reaching, then, a twilight zone: the twilight of desire.

—Erik Pevernagie

We know that if we eat a certain food, it will upset our digestion, but we still eat it. The way out is to be aware of the superficial appearance. From outside, something may look very pleasant. But we have to look deeper and use that deep understanding to see the superficial aspects of the object of our desire. Our understandings can overcome our cravings.

—Thich Nhat Hanh

Standing at the observation deck, you see a friend climbing on to a rollercoaster ride. She had asked you to join but you didn't see the fun and thrill in it. As the ride starts and the speed increases, the rollercoaster twisting and turning, you hear the people screaming and bellowing from their seats, some even shrieking and begging for it to stop. You observe mesmerized, shaking your head at times, unable to fathom the need those others have that tempts them to do what they are doing—seeking gratification by facing grave danger instead of deriving joy from their daily existence. You feel disconnected. Not too many people you know see it the way you do. Many who don't ride refrain because they feel nauseous and sick, not because they don't get it the way you do.

People Seek Fun and Stimulation

We are designed to have fun. We seek stimulation. It comes to us as naturally as breathing or sleeping. Seeking fun and happiness helps people thrive. This is true even in the most debilitating circumstances. It allows people to cope with stressful situations, to build resilience and work their way through adversities. In continuing to maintain the idea of seeking and having fun while negotiating the spaces one occupies, it creates the opportunity to feel well and healthy, promoting the overall quality of life.

It is through seeking fun that people also learn to relax and cope with the stress that they may experience in their life. By preventing the building up of overwhelming thoughts and emotions and promoting a balanced life, it allows them to reflect and introspect, to find creative solutions to the experiences they have and the situations they face. Through engaging in fun and seeking stimulation, people are able to enhance their learning in situations.

All of these benefits naturally predispose people to seek fun and stimulation in the way they live their life. Many wonder about their days as young children when they engaged with their environment and explored spaces freely, running around without inhibition and doing the things they liked in exactly the way they liked. The memories of that adrenalin rush they experienced in their early years can be rather tempting.

As adults, working one's way through the rules and norms of society and workplaces, people learn to reign in that free-spirited manner in which they engaged with their environment as children. The seeking of fun becomes largely contingent upon performance. The achievement of goals becomes a prerequisite for being able to experience fun and stimulation. In your adolescent years, you would have been told, 'If you want to go out and play, first finish all your work.' In your adult years, at work, you were perhaps told, 'You can't get leave this week. There is a lot of work pending for your team.' In these and many other ways, the natural drive to seek fun is curbed. Yet, it persists subconsciously and drives much behaviour displayed by people.

The Need for Instant Gratification

We live in an environment where most things are available a click away. We live lives in which waiting and patience is a much coveted yet a less available virtue. People find themselves a little less concerned with the long-term consequences and more often driven by what is or can be done in the short term. They seek the immediate gratification of their needs. They want what they want at the time that they desire it. Waiting and hanging on in the fringes, so to say, is not a desirable state. Ending the misery of waiting tends to drive much of how people often behave across diverse situations.

There is a strong need to run away from the uncertainties of living a life. Predictability is the preferred mode of existence. Delays in anything are best avoided as one doesn't want to be denied any opportunity or benefit that can be accrued soon. As a result, an impulsive lifestyle gets rewarded that fails to take into account the long-term consequences of the actions undertaken by a person.

These contribute to the temptation to engage in actions that would lead to an immediate release of the stressors you experience. You may feel tempted to consider easy alternatives that give you that instant sense of gratification. The cravings for these can be strong and you may feel drawn to try out something that is different from the conventional ways of relaxing and enjoying.

Numbing Away the Stress

The stress of living the life you do can be rather overwhelming. Living a life, making ends meet, moving towards life's luxuries, having beautiful desirable relationships, can all make you feel stressed. This constant pressure of keeping up with what is expected from you, what you expect from yourself and idealized notions of how life is supposed to be, do not permit relief from the stress you feel. It can be a rather inhibiting experience, making you feel caged and trapped in a vicious circle at times.

It can be tempting to find ways to release this stress. You may want to numb all that pain and excessive thinking you indulge in. You may have heard of how substances* can help with this—making you feel numb, not letting you experience anything bad in those moments of indulgence. This all too tempting idea may get support from your friends and colleagues. You may even be closely associated with those who frequently experiment. They goad you into being experimental—after all, what can be the harm in trying just once.

The day you do try it, you think you feel different. The seed for further experimentation has germinated. It is difficult to not loop back to all these temptations. You perhaps find yourself getting pulled into the vortex of this lifestyle.

Disconnect from the Pressure and Strains

Sometimes you feel that all you need is a break. Your mind needs to stop running and the job and people in your life need to be less demanding. You want to be able to step away from your responsibilities and revel in the spirit of being free. There is a temptation to disconnect from everything around—you feel that it would let you relax, unwind and feel rejuvenated so that you can come back all charged up to take on more.

You have heard it being said that indulging in substances, dabbling a bit and experimenting with them can help you experience that disconnection. Your friends may have mentioned that you would be able to feel a calm state in

---

*By substances we refer to any form in which these may exist, including and not restricted to cigarettes, alcohol and psychoactive drugs.

which you can be oblivious to what goes on around you. You may find it possible to actually disconnect and not feel worried about all the things that you need to work on and all the problems that you need to resolve.

Your mind can see this as an opportunity to be able to disconnect while remaining connected. The notion of momentarily being able to mentally disconnect without causing disruption to your work or relationships can be rather alluring.

Relaxation May Get Amplified

Many falsely assume that the consumption of these substances would lead to heightened states of relaxation and even happiness. They feel that the experiences that can be accrued in such moments are irreplaceable. Your day-to-day life, it is believed, does not have the bandwidth to provide the opportunity for such feeling states—regular days are no match for these experiences.

There is a desire to exist in a blissfully relaxed state. When you see or hear someone comment about how relaxed they feel, you too feel drawn towards it. Resisting these alluring moments is hard. Your mind questions, 'Isn't this what you always wanted? Didn't you desire that you should be able to relax, enjoy, be happy and free of all worries?' When you don't find any convincing answers that you trust, your defences get breached. It is in such moments that you can get pushed over by someone else or your own mind to try and experiment just this once.

It is easy for your mind to convince you. You think, 'What's the harm in trying once?' You feel forced to experience the relaxation the first time you get swayed. Even if it did nothing for you, you feel like you must go back—maybe second time it will work like a charm. And before you know it, it has become a part of your routine.

Dependence Skyrockets

The thing with any and all substances is that outside of your conscious awareness, they insidiously take hold of you. You may not even recognize it and your dependency on their continued availability and usage increases. From the scenario when you first used a substance in a controlled manner to regulate how you felt, things shift drastically to the emergence of a situation where the substance now controls you. You may struggle to regulate how much of it you use and consume. When you are in the midst of difficult or stressful situations, your mind keeps veering towards considering consuming something. Most of this happens in the hope of stoking that calm, relaxed, disconnected state you experienced the first time. But that no longer happens.

In contrast, what does happen is that you can feel the changes in your mood states even as you attempt to modulate them by indulging in a substance of your choice. You feel moody and temperamental, snapping at people around you, feeling irritated with small things. Your desire to be left alone can get heightened, making you react negatively to others around you. You can feel your focus drifting away and the choices you need to make for your life becoming more difficult.

Even as you go through these transitions, their slow

acting nature can be deceptive. You may not even see the link between these aspects. You may believe, instead, that it's all happening because you are getting tired and exhausted, being sucked into problems, getting stuck in unresolvable patterns.

Conflicts Are a By-Product

As you go through these changes and transitions, those around you are likely to see the transformations. Besides, there are likely to be members in your family and maybe even in your social network who feel concerned about your well-being. Seeing you getting stuck in a pattern, consuming substances of any form, is difficult for them to process. Their care and concern for you make them reach out to you repeatedly, even though you may fail to see that there is a problem.

Their uneasiness and reservations about your choices make you feel that there is distrust and doubt. It riles you internally to know that they consider your choices disputable. Their reluctance to trust you makes you angry. This, you feel, is a reflection of the historicity of your relationship with them. That is, maybe, what has always prevented you from flying and soaring to great heights. It all can feel rather convoluted in your head.

The end by-product is immense, escalating conflict. It all started out because you wanted peace, calm and happiness. What you are left with is discord and disharmony in the relationships that have been central to your life.

A Square Peg in a Round Hole

These emerging scenarios can make you feel like a square peg in a round hole. The disconnect which you needed from the hectic, frenzied way of living has rampantly grown and extended its arms across other domains of your life. From the moments of peace and solitude that you sought, you have perhaps reached a place where many relationships are compromised. The work that drove you to do more and achieve more also stands imperilled.

You may find yourself struggling to fit in and be a part of anything that seems substantive and in consonance with what you seek. Perhaps you also aren't certain anymore of what you really want. Confusion laces the activities, work and relationships that typifies your existence. It can make you question your very core. The result is not comforting in any manner. It infuriates you, distresses you and disappoints you.

We Need to Look at the Long Term

The necessary expedient strategy that needs to be put into play involves giving due consideration to the implications of your chosen actions to the life you yearn for in the long run. Losing sight of this fundamental and decisive aspect is not an option. To ensure the acquisition of your life goals you cannot afford to get derailed. You need to have minor considerations of what works in the immediate short term. Any approach you adopt must consider how it contributes or takes away from where you want to be in the long run. Despite how difficult it may appear to conceptualize this as an approach, it can certainly be integrated into your ways of living by being more mindfully engaged to your own self, your goals and your vision.

10

GADGET-O-MANIA

There are times when I have to take, I call it a 'silence bath,' where I shut off all of the external gadgets. I go walk around, talk to people and just live life for a while.

—Patton Oswalt

Don't let a busy life or electronic communication gadgets be your excuse for excess solitude—it's a talent, but a rare one, to make yourself laugh.

—Mireille Guiliano

Humanity is acquiring all the right technology for all the wrong reasons.

—R. Buckminster Fuller

Sitting with your family at the dinner table you may wonder how things have changed. From the time when it was the space for conversations and staying connected with each other's lives, it has become merely a table. Conversations barely happen. Your partner wants to quickly run back to the television to catch a glimpse of the match that is running or hear the news that is playing. Your children want to get back to their phones—texting their friends and being cued to what is going on in social media is the most important thing, it seems. Even as you prod all of them, seeking an insight into how their day was, all you get are perfunctory cursory responses. It almost feels like they don't want to be disturbed. You sigh, drop your head and, looking at your plate, get back to eating.

Staying Connected to the World

As social beings, there is a strong need for us to remain connected to all that goes on in the lives of those one feels connected to. This is strongly supported by the great technological advancements that have been made in recent decades. Social media platforms support this entrenched desire to know and be informed. People spend increasing amounts of time on these platforms—connecting with those they actually know and also with those who they would like to know. You don't restrict yourself to getting in touch with those you know personally or professionally. You may even find yourself attempting to get acquainted with others who you don't know. Then, there is the additional desire to be privy to the lives of your role models—celebrities from different walks of life whose lives appear rather desirable.

Being acquainted with and having complete information about the lives of others can be a big temptation. It is usually seen to stem from a dual need. On the one hand, you may not want to come across as being disinterested and uninvolved with the lives of those you are supposed to be closely associated with—friends, colleagues or family. On the other hand, you also don't want to miss out on the things they may be doing. Somewhere, underlying this second aspect, may also be a parallel thought process that pushes you to make constant comparisons. It allows you to know what the other person is doing, how they are doing it, what are the various things that comprise their life today and how they are distinct from the life you are leading. It acts as a motivator. Sometimes it even creates a sense of wanting more—wanting that very thing, the life that the other person has.

You may even find yourself replacing the real interactions you could have had with people with connections over social media instead. In place of choosing to call someone, you may prefer to exchange notes over text. Instead of going to their place to ask them how they are, you may just call them to check in with them. Somewhere, the real conversations which set apart the relationship you may have had with people gets relegated to the background.

There are mountains of information that you can consume. Sifting through, sorting and reaching a place of understanding about what may be most relevant and important, which you need to focus on, can be hard. It can quickly become unmanageable and before you know it, instead of being informed about what goes on, you are rather uninformed about most things which may be of importance.

The Missing Content and Context

Despite all the connection we derive from social media platforms and the gadgets we use, we somewhere stay disconnected. The biggest problem that has resulted from these advancements has been the growing feeling of loneliness that many report in spite of the ability to reach to more number of people and to be connected with them. Even in being 'friends' with thousands of others you may feel disconnected and alone. Having friends on social media doesn't translate into you feeling supported or cared for. It does not reflect in the availability of someone you can turn to in case you find yourself struggling.

The advent of technology has certainly resulted in you collecting numerous friends. But there is no guarantee for the quality of these relationships or the extent to which you can genuinely connect with them. The context of your association may not involve much in common. There is a high likelihood that you may not have contacted them outside of these platforms. You would have perhaps never thought twice about many of these people who would have remained your acquaintances and whose life's details you would have been unaware of.

Somewhere, it is more pleasurable to be bombarded with those limited characters which another person utilizes to express what they are thinking. It is easier to palate these than to have a full-flowing conversation with them. You too, keep extending yourself out there, placing content in the form of statements, narratives, videos and images—some of them real, others created, to have an impact on those who view and consume them.

Projecting an Image Is Important

Most people hold in their minds a notion of how they would like to be perceived by others. They have ideas about who they are and how they tend to be in their relationships as well as in their responses to situations. They wish to be perceived in accordance with these inherently held ideas and, for that to happen, they are also tempted to project a certain image across all their social media platforms.

Content is created that is specifically geared towards ensuring its concordance with this closely held self-image. You may also discover, in the process, that you are often with your devices, ensuring that you are documenting relevant parts of your life. Staying with these gadgets and being attached to others through these media may be a preferred mode of operating. It reduces those uncomfortable conversations. It gives the freedom to shape how others perceive and think of you. It creates an opportunity to determine exactly how the world views and understands you.

The temptation to exert this control over what is perceived is rather strong. It is difficult to simply ignore it and let it be. You are also subconsciously aware of the same mechanisms that others are using to impact how you view them. It can almost feel like a cyclical, never-ending game.

No Fomo for Me

Unknowingly, without your conscious awareness, there is a hidden element that operates behind the amount of time you spend on your gadgets and on social media. It is not that you seek connections alone. You also don't want to be left alone. You don't want to be the person who is unaware and caught off guard in a conversation or not knowing what is being discussed.

There is a strong fear of missing out that operates somewhere at the back of your mind. It unconsciously drives much of your behaviour. It can feel almost compulsive in nature. The manner in which you constantly pick up your gadget and automatically go to check out your social media platforms or consistently stare at the screen of your computer or television, is seemingly automatic and does not involve much conscious thinking being directed towards it.

Moreover, you do not want to be the odd one out who is always checking with others to know what is going on or what it was that you missed. It can feel embarrassing. There is an unsaid expectation from those you are associated with that you would be fairly attuned to what they put out there. So, it is not just your need which is pushing you to be on your devices continually. It is also the perceived pressure and expectation from others that drives this aspect of your behaviour till it becomes a habituated pattern of being.

There Is an Information Overload

You cannot exert much control over what type of and how much information comes your way through the gadgets you use. Even if you seek less, you are likely to be bombarded with enormous content. It is like a wave that keeps crashing against you, relentless in its trajectory, constantly coming back at you even if you want to try and run away from it.

It is exhilarating to think of having everything at your command, easy to access and acquire. Yet, it can be rather overwhelming because there is just so much that you can consume. What started out as a convenient way of staying updated has somewhere also perhaps become an anxiety-provoking mechanism. Despite your best efforts, you are likely to find yourself lagging behind. There is no point at which you can think, 'Ok, now I know it all. I don't need to look at it or search any further.' There is no end to the extent to which you can inform yourself.

This, somewhere, also affects your real-life interactions because, in attempting to stay on top of the information you need to consume, you spend lesser time in engaging with those who are around you. How often is it that you see a couple out for dinner and both of them are busy looking at their phones? Or how common is it for a friend or a family member to be rather distracted by their device even as you are speaking with them?

Restless without My Gadgets

Imagine a situation where you don't have your phone, iPad or laptop with you. You need to be without any access to these devices that have become such an integral part of your life. It may be difficult for you to easily conjure this image in your mind and find the activities that you would do to pass your entire day. This thought, in itself, may make you feel uneasy, unsure and perhaps even anxious and worried about how it would be possible for you to just be and not have a device that you can flick on and use to distract yourself.

That is what the various gadgets you use have primarily become—a strong source of distraction. They take you away from the people and situations that you face. More importantly, they take you away from your troublesome thoughts and feelings. Staying with these is often difficult and perplexing. They constantly highlight the problems of your life and the things you need to do. The emotions keep bringing to mind what bothers you. You must have noticed that, unfortunately, the mind is not primed to assess things that make you feel happy and good. Instead, it has a penchant for veering in the direction of those elements that are disturbing and need fixing.

So you gravitate towards your devices in an automatic fashion. In a reflexive manner you reach out for one of them as soon as you feel there isn't much that is engaging you in your current environment. When you feel bored or the conversations around you are stress inducing, you immediately reach out for one of your gadgets.

We Can Circumvent the Disconnection

The yin of technology and gadgets is also associated with a corresponding yang that can skew the balance in the direction of the negative. In an immensely connected world, there is a strong current of disconnection that also flows beneath the surface, facilitated by the gadgets we rely on. This disconnection can be with people, with the environment, with our interests and with our hobbies. Circumventing this disconnection is a possibility. But it requires us to reassess and re-evaluate the processes of our engagement. It necessarily requires that we reconsider our way of utilizing these stellar technological advances and how we integrate them into our daily lives. It means becoming more consciously aware of what we are doing and how we are doing it.

11

THE EVASIVE OUTDOORS

I would rather be amongst forest animals and the sounds of nature, than amongst city traffic and the noise of man.

—Anthony Douglas Williams

In every walk with nature one receives far more than he seeks.

—John Muir

In all things of nature there is something of the marvellous.

—Aristotle

As you stand on the sidelines watching your child being coached in the technicalities of playing a game of tennis, you detect yourself reflecting on your own past. You go down memory lane reminiscing about the times you would play different games and sports—badminton, cricket, volleyball, and even football. Most of these would involve your peers and you mutually formulating rules and discovering skills and strategies of engaging with different ways of playing and being outdoors. There was no structure to the play and no adults who would supervise. The primary motive was to have fun and to just be outdoors. How well you played and who was winning were a secondary concern or perhaps even no concern at all.

A Natural Inclination for Unstructured Time

In our journey towards not being scattered and being productive, we have been working consistently with great diligence and commitment, to making our lives structured. We dedicatedly work towards building routines. We set in place rules about when to wake up, when to get ready, when to start our work, when to end it, when we should be stepping out and when we can engage with recreational activities. All of this structure helps us feel in control. The ambiguity of daily life can otherwise become quite overwhelming. The stress of it all can be unmanageable.

Even as we seek to create this structure, sometimes it can make us feel stifled and constrained. The knowledge that you need to stick to a set pattern of doing, being and behaving can be draining and exhausting. Herein lies the significant role and position that is occupied by unstructured time in our lives. Not having a specific purpose attached to the time you have can be very helpful. It can become the time in a day when you don't have to be worried about what has to come next and what task you need to finish at a given time.

This unstructured time allows your creative juices to flow. It can be that period in the day when you can allow yourself to come up with unique, novel thoughts and ideas. This is when you can just be and give yourself the chance to recharge yourself. You can ready yourself for the next day or the next week and come back to the things that you need to do with a completely restored and renewed sense of energy. It allows you to be able to approach situations, both old and new, with a different and fresh perspective.

Not having any expectations from yourself during this period of unstructured time can be a substantial relief from the rigmarole of everyday life. Not having to satisfy the demands of others, your work or your personal living is a unique experience. You can feel free to do anything, be any way and do things at a pace that works for you. This, more importantly, gives you the time to reflect and introspect, and to determine whether the manner in which you have been managing things is working well for you or not. The fast-paced life you lead otherwise may not accord you the opportunity to determine whether what and how you are doing things is working well for you and enabling the achievement of your personal goals.

Revelling in this unstructured time is something most humans desire. It is the lack of experimentation with it over the years that can make it difficult to consider it with seriousness. Its value evades us especially because we have not given it that importance. Yet, it remains considerably significant and accords massive benefits if you can find the courage and just learn to be. Utilizing it to step outdoors, doing and experimenting with activities outside of your home and office space is rather beneficial.

Free Time Is Not Unstructured Time

It is easy to assume that the free time you have is equivalent to having unstructured time. The difference between the two can be hard to enumerate upon. Nevertheless, there is a marked point of divergence between the two. Your free time is that which you can utilize for activities or work that you have in mind or that you need to do. In contrast, your unstructured time is a period of your free time when you don't have anything planned.

When you keep your free time unstructured, time can slip by in a flash. You may not even realize and hours can go by, leaving you feeling as though you did not do anything or accomplish much. Staying with this realization can be difficult. Your experiences growing up have not encouraged you to value such a time during the day or the week when you do nothing specific. You have always been encouraged to have a contingency plan in place that allows you to keep being consistently productive.

Deterred by Goal Directedness

This natural desire for unstructured time, to be able to step outdoors and do something or do absolutely nothing, is often deterred on account of the reinforced need to be goal-directed. Pushed by your learning across socialization experiences, you know it is important to have a set of goals you unfailingly work towards.

Besides being stuck to your workspace even when you are at home with family or friends, your mind conceivably gets directed towards finding something concrete to do that relates to the larger goals you have. In being this way, you may struggle to prioritize being outdoors, finding unstructured time or engaging in activities that give you real pleasure and help you relax and unwind.

The very goal directedness which is most certainly an asset when it comes to being an achiever, becomes a deterring factor in this respect. It has an inhibitory effect which interferes with being able to step outside. You keep thinking and feeling like you just don't have the time or that you would rather utilize the time that you do have to do the things that are necessary to leading that 'good life'.

Inhibited by the Environment

It is natural to feel concerned about the weather and the quality of the air that you would be breathing if you were to step outdoors. Most feel concerned about it being either too hot or too cold. Often, the weather can be rather unpredictable and it is hard to determine where you can go, what clothes you must wear and how long you can be out. If there is too much pollution, then you most certainly don't want to be outside and expose your body to hazardous fumes.

It then becomes easier to simplify things and, instead, schedule them in a way that there is least exposure to uncertainties and maximum control over environment-related factors. So you may then choose to join classes that involve exercise and activities which are primarily run indoors. It allows you to keep things running as per your timings and schedules and also allows you to be able to feel more in control of factors that could prohibit you from following through with them.

Driven by your desire to ensure that you don't face the disappointment of having to reschedule or cancel something because of environmental factors, you increasingly inhibit your forays outdoors. More of your activities get restricted to the home, a gym, an activity centre or your workplace.

We Can Find a Way to Re-Engage with Our Childhood

Re-engaging with your childhood is a real possibility. You can take steps to become more involved with nature and the natural environment. You don't always need to schedule those long hikes and holidays to be able to step outdoors. It's a choice that you can make to find ways to be outdoors daily or some time every week or at any other place that works for you. You don't have to be a desk jockey. In fact, it would be wonderful for you if you aren't. To enjoy, to be able to actualize your creative potential, you need to find a way to integrate the outdoors into your routines.

Section II

Sectie II

Take Stock

Take stock: To carefully think about something in order to make a decision about what to do next

You now know there is a problem. It presents itself as a constellation of different constituent elements that uniquely impinge upon your life. Whether you feel prepared or not, you must find the courage to contend with it. Even as you feel vulnerable and exposed, you need to take that next step. The point you must start at is to ask yourself that all-important question, 'What should I do next?' Seemingly simple, this is perhaps one of the biggest questions you would struggle to answer at different stages of your life.

Finding that next step can be difficult—it is a monumental decision on which rests much of what will follow. The challenge, as is evident, is beyond arriving at alternatives. It resides as much in accumulating the relevant facts, weaving them into a coherent whole, determining the point at which you need to start and having a fair degree of certainty about the appropriateness of the approach and the benefits that can be accrued by adopting it in the long run.

This process of deliberating about that next step will have many pitfalls along its path. It can certainly be arduous and unnerving. There will be no clearly demarcated right and wrong, nothing that would be able to tell you, 'This is the absolute right path'. You would need to be willing to take your chances, manage the anxiety as it emerges whilst you make your choices. You may feel overwhelmed with the number of things you need to consider. It may appear to be too much and too taxing. You may want to withdraw. You may feel tempted to hide away and not have to do any decision-making. You may want to stop the problem-solving but you know that, having made the progress that you have, stepping back is not the best course of action.

Be Curious

Having made the journey this far, having discovered the things that are a bother, you may need that extra push to find the energy to prioritize and bring your curiosity to the fore. Even as you understand its value in helping you know, understand, learn, remember, grow, engage and be passionate, it can be an elusive concept that may cause a strain in applying. You will find growth, contentment and happiness in staying connected and engaged, and in knowing what you need.

To find solutions that are creative and give a unique answer to the challenges you have identified, you need to be curious. You can find your mind flourishing with ideas as you seek more inputs. To find the path towards improvements and enhanced quality of living, curiosity can act as the conduit towards innovation.

This curiosity, nevertheless can often evade you. Even as you make a determined effort, it may be easier to find your shell and bury yourself in it. Sticking to what is familiar is always more comfortable. It would certainly reduce the chances of experiencing any form of disruption in your life. But it would also take away from the possibility of discovering something new, something old, something that can bring a fresh perspective and also something that can change your expectations and add meaning to your life.

Letting go of the fear that can quell your curiosity can be difficult. Harbouring thoughts of disappointment and dejection can take away from the chances of you experimenting to reach a fresh and novel understanding. The intrinsic motivation you can derive from being curious can be completely lost if you don't push and strive for looking within and looking out to explore and discover.

Succumbing to the anxiety of feeling lost and losing your grip on maintaining your curiosity is a real possibility. But you can strive to maintain it by working to find the things that pique your interest and fascinate you. Trying something different and something new, albeit at the risk of provoking your anxiety, can still help you maintain the spirit of being curious. This practice of being curious across diverse domains is sure to contribute towards it being more easily applied to the next steps you need to take in the broader framework of your life. This emerges because of the potential for it to become a part of your natural predisposition.

Reworking Old Habits

A pattern of thinking and responding that is steeped in curiosity may not come to you naturally. Yet, it certainly is an approach that you can cultivate. As you strive to find your answers, you can make a more concerted, conscious effort to be aware, issuing reminders to your mind to be curious. As you continue to explore your surroundings with an open mind, you come to realize that curiosity can find its place and seep into your subconscious way of responding to situations and towards people as well.

Habits once formed are not averse to change. The onus lies on you to take ownership, bring consciousness and plunge yourself into this effortful approach. It does not come easy for sure, but the dividends it can get you in the long run can be enormous. You may feel apprehensive and worry about the possibility of incurring costs on account of challenging the status quo you are comfortably settled in. However, this curiosity ensures that you do not settle down for the first possible solution that you come up with. The exploration allows you to take stock of all available alternatives (as many as you possibly can) and not be restricted to an automatic, habituated mode of thinking and responding.

It is not that you need to unlearn. You need to consider this process as one that involves reworking and altering your learning. It is a process that is oriented towards your personal development. Every new idea will not lead to your growth, but it can act as a springboard towards other new and better ones, those that may just allow you to fix the problems you have identified.

Looking Ahead

The key lies in looking ahead. Having a prospective approach is going to be a boon towards finding effective solutions. It is easy to get stuck in the past. Getting bogged down due to past experiences, more so the failures and lack of successful plans, is always a grave possibility. You may find your mind rushing back and forth, attempting to gather together all evidence pointing towards the problems you have experienced or potentially could experience due to the new approach.

That is how the human mind can often function. It wants to avoid threats and threatening situations. It strives to find solutions to problems it imagines could potentially emerge in the future. Keeping yourself motivated and driven can be difficult in such a situation. As you grapple with worries about what can be or get stuck with the things that have been in the past, you may find it difficult to stay in the moment and make the moves towards the future.

However, despite all the tricks that your mind can curate, staying on the path of finding your solutions is certainly possible. Pushing yourself to keep looking ahead is required. And that would involve you being able to recognize and remember what you seek. Redirecting your mind towards this goal is the mechanism which needs to be instated. In the following chapters, we will look at the precise methods through which this mechanism can be brought into play and implemented to ensure that you are able to combat the loneliness you experience in your life.

12

ACKNOWLEDGE THE PROBLEM

Knowing is not enough; we must apply. Willing is not enough; we must do.

—Johann Wolfgang von Goethe

You cannot solve a problem until you acknowledge that you have one and accept responsibility for solving it.

—Zig Ziglar

When a problem arises, don't fight with it or try to deny it. Accept and acknowledge it. Be patient in seeking a solution or opening, and then fully commit yourself to the resolution you think advisable.

—Joe Hyams

Rummaging around in your kitchen, trying to fix a meal for yourself, you can feel a burden on your chest. You know there are things that bother you, yet you fear having to see them, segregate them and figure out exactly what is causing you to feel this way. Even as you come close to determining what troubles you, you want to run away, pick the phone and call someone, find a distraction, something that will prevent you from knowing. You don't want to reach the knowledge of what is troubling you, even as you know that you must. It is far more simple and enticing to drift away into a different world where you remain unfettered by those things, the scary thoughts and realizations that are brewing under the surface, edging closer to the brim, getting ready to rise and flood your reality. Acknowledging there is a problem is just such a struggle.

Ignorance Is Not Bliss

In striving to be happy and live a fulfilling life, you can find yourself drifting in the direction of embracing ignorance. You may believe that in caring less about things, situations, relationships and the problems you perceive in them, you can protect yourself from feeling a plethora of negative emotions. You may consider that dealing with these extensive negative pieces can pull you down, take away your drive and focus, not let you be progressive in your approach and burden you unnecessarily. But you forget that even as you attempt to be largely ignorant, things do continue to brew under the surface. They operate in your subconscious and keep influencing and shaping your expectations and responses. They impact your moods and alter how you think. Even as you think you have escaped, you end up being stuck in their clutches.

This 'don't worry, be happy' mindset can become the reason for your unravelling. As you attempt to be unconcerned about your environment and the problems that may exist for you, you can begin to feel like you live an artificially constructed life. Your actions are contingent upon the mindset you possess, and being in a state of ignorance doesn't let you acknowledge the problems you have. This results in not being able to take the requisite actions and steps to solve the problems that do exist. Ultimately, it leads to a scenario where things build up and become unmanageable and the more you attempt to run away from them, the more they follow you.

Achieving real fulfilment and satisfaction in life involves being aware of and acknowledging the problems that exist. You may desire that childhood state where the presence of others was sufficient to meet your needs. But it cannot change the reality of you having to take charge today. Not having to take responsibility or being unaware of the various complexities of life and the challenges it brings with it is not a viable option.

The sooner you acknowledge the presence of problems, the more likely you are to reach a state where you feel a degree of certitude and calm. In acknowledging problems, you bring a sense of control by reducing the anxiety of not knowing and being ignorant. It may sound paradoxical and yet it is the most helpful and effective way to be.

Flooding Is Not the Answer

Breaking past the ignorance you may have been living with does not have to translate into the absolute extreme opposite of flooding yourself. The information you may have been ignorant of—sometimes passively and at other times actively—cannot be brought forth all together and all of a sudden. While information is our biggest, most valued commodity, it doesn't help to get flooded with it. Such an approach can cause serious and severe disruption in well-being, decision-making, problem-solving, as well as productivity, across the different domains of life.

The reason for this is that if you open the floodgates too soon or too quickly, the ability to process all the information gets compromised. It overwhelms and leaves you feeling depleted. It leaves your mind feeling confused and unsure, making it difficult to take the first step towards analysing the information you have received to make it into a coherent whole, insights from which can be applied by you. It also contributes to increased distractibility as each new set of information that reaches you has the potential to attract your attention.

Instead, there is a method to decoding it all that involves a careful deconstruction and peeling away of the layers of ignorance. This may seem difficult to conceptualize, but what it means is that the elements you have avoided engaging with need to be approached one at a time, at a steady consistent pace.

Ready for a Strategy

So what you do need is a strategy to be put in place so that the information overload does not get to you and paralyse you. We would look at these across the subsequent chapters. But first things first—you need to start with getting ready to create a strategy. Putting yourself in the right frame of mind is important and this is critical to the process of acknowledging the problem as well. This right frame of mind can be set in place by recognizing the value of what you are setting yourself up to do. Being aware of the purpose, value and meaning of the need to work on the problems you see in how you are living is helpful.

This means you need to prioritize and give more importance to solving this problem of loneliness that you are experiencing. Distancing yourself from it, dismissing it or neglecting its presence is not an option. The more you do so, the larger it is going to become. You must ask yourself the following questions to be able to see the value of the journey you are about to embark upon:

- What was the life I envisioned growing up and where am I today?
- What is it that matters most to me today?
- What is it that is missing from where I wanted to be?
- How can I enhance my personal sense of accomplishment?

As you recognize the value of what you are endeavouring to do—tackling the loneliness you experience in your life—you will find the drive to not put off the tasks you need to engage with in order to make the changes and shifts within yourself and your approach.

Letting Go of Control

Bringing change means letting go of control. It means allowing yourself to be vulnerable. It involves being ready to accept failure. This failure is what leads to learning and developing a better understanding. You must show great courage in being able to take these steps to transform your life as it involves letting go of that control you perhaps would love to have.

No individual likes making a choice for which the outcomes may not be in their control. There will be no foolproof mechanism to determine the efficacy or effectiveness of the changes you herald into your life. There is a possibility that some things you try will succeed and others may not be all that successful. There would be some aspects that may turn out to be an outright failure. Tolerating this, and not allowing it to impact your assessment of who you are, how good enough you are and whether you can foster the agency to bring about this change, is important.

You need to be comfortable with relinquishing your need for control. You must revel in the journey of experimentation and discovery. You would need to be ready to step away from your natural manner of responding to situations and try approaches which do not fully resonate with you. In disruption, you will find solutions that will allow you to reach a unique solution.

We All Have Limited Cognitive Resources

Every individual has limited cognitive resources to keep looking at, absorbing, processing and deriving meaning from the information coming their way. If you do feel overwhelmed once in a while, refrain from unleashing judgments upon yourself. You can slow down, take a break and decide to step away to get back to things at a later point in time. There is no fixed, precise way to go about doing things and engaging in this process of change and transformation. Embrace your journey, enjoy it, revel in it and make accommodations for your fatigue and exhaustion.

Don't push yourself to a point of feeling like you will collapse. Maintain an even pace and keep taking steady steps in the direction you need to keep going in. Be willing to take a break. Make conscious efforts to integrate them into your routines so you don't reach the point where you feel like you are burning out. Set the right boundaries for yourself by asking questions like, 'Am I doing too much?' 'Am I taking too much responsibility?' 'Are my needs getting met?' and 'Am I getting too overwhelmed?'

Don't Internalize Others' Emotions

A word of caution is warranted at this point. You must make a concerted effort to ensure that you do not subconsciously keep absorbing and internalizing the emotions of other people around you. As you move in the direction of change, it is likely to create discomfort for people who surround you. They may feel uneasy and would perhaps need to readjust themselves. This can potentially push you to reconsider what you are doing.

In reconsidering, do not give up entirely on what you need to do. You can tweak your approach and make adjustments. But be mindful about staying cognizant of what your needs are in this scenario and the problems that you need to address. In being satisfied and content with the changes you make, you will also find it leading to more positive influences on your relationships. So, despite the initial resistance of people around you, they will eventually be able to see the benefits of your new approach as you continue to stay committed to your journey of transformation.

Giving Happens with Contentment

To give to your relationships, you need to be in a happier place yourself. Contentment with yourself and your life will let you be a giver in your relationships. Generosity will thus come from being able to find contentment in your life as it will permit you to be an authentic giver—not one who does so at the cost of the self, but one who does so in a way that it does not allow resentment and anger to breed within their relationships.

13

KNOWING IS THE FIRST STEP

Knowing yourself is the beginning of all wisdom.

—Aristotle

The art of knowing is knowing what to ignore.

—Rumi

Do the difficult things while they're easy and do the great things while they're small. A journey of a thousand miles must begin with a single step.

—Lao Tzu

You sit in front of your computer. The result for your interview is going to be shared. You feel hesitant in opening your inbox. It provokes enormous anxiety. Even though you are eager to know how it went, you find your mind overwhelmed by distinct images of what the interview was like. You replay all the questions in your mind and how you answered them. It unnerves you to think of the possibility of not making it through. It feels like such an important interview. It is a golden opportunity you most certainly want to cash in on. Yet, you don't want to know what the end result is. Delving into the process seems like such a scary thought.

Taking the First Step

As Lao Tzu once said, 'A journey of a thousand miles begins with a single step.' But taking that treacherous first step can feel very difficult. Determining the right approach usually becomes a necessity and an expectation. You feel that taking a step that pushes you in the wrong direction is best avoidable. You wouldn't want to feel like you wasted time. No one wants to retrace their steps. At the end of the day, when you take the time to reflect, you want to feel accomplished.

Worry can arise if you end up feeling like you missed a step or took the wrong step. You can get stuck because the fear of not making it grips you tightly. You have apprehensions about making an effort and it getting wasted, and that pulls you away from exposing yourself. It doesn't permit you to let yourself be vulnerable, to take that risk and just plunge yourself into the situation to try and see if things can work out well for you.

What you end up doing is then postpone taking any action. You wait for time to pass and keep mulling over the alternatives you see. The more you look at them, the more you feel confused. Your mind can feel absolutely boggled because it has lost track of where you'd started from and where you are now. The confusion also results in irritation. It makes you feel upset and distressed. Anger can flow through you as you struggle to make the decision to take that first step.

Yet, you must take the first step. Unlike what most believe, the first step is not about taking action. It's towards building understanding and equipping yourself with the right knowledge. The process of knowing is irreplaceable as that quintessential first step in the journey towards overcoming this loneliness which is seeping into our very existence and becoming a rather prominent part of our lives.

Ask Questions

You must start where you are. And you must start by asking questions—the same questions answers to which you might fear and be apprehensive about. Finding the courage to receive the answers is a necessity and it starts by being willing to take that all-important first step. Once you find the will to go forward, you start by asking the simple question, 'Where all do I identify the problem?'

Identifying and defining the problem allows you to be able to start determining the steps you need to take. Concurrently, determining the aspects that cause you to experience the most fear and apprehension contributes to developing an understanding of the issues you may need to tackle before you get down to solving the problems.

In asking questions, you are often likely to realize that the things that are causing you stress or making you feel anxious have no real basis to them. You are able to recognize that a lot of what you are experiencing is a result of the mind running in different directions, feeling overwhelmed, and as a result you are unsure about what you need to do and how you must respond to the situation.

Given that you have an understanding of the areas which can cause you to feel an enhanced sense of loneliness in this urban life, knowing and breaking it down into its specific constituent parts can happen by asking the right questions. The other questions you should consider asking yourself are:

- What is the goal I am working towards?
- What are the elements which hold maximum meaning for me?
- What is it that I want to achieve in my personal and professional spaces?
- What are the possible sources of hindrance to reaching my goals?
- What are the aspects I can control and which are the ones beyond my control?

Acquire More Information

To be able to answer the questions you generate, you may realize that you need some more information. It is helpful to consider and consult multiple sources to be able to have a holistic understanding. Restricting yourself to what your mind says can contribute to the creation of a bias. It is difficult for your mind to be able to come up with multiple aspects, different facets and perspectives all on its own.

Simultaneously, even as you identify one area that you feel may need focused attention from you to help in resolving the situation you find yourself in, it's important that you elaborate upon it. Further defining it and elucidating upon its varying components will allow you to have a more robust understanding that is comprehensive in itself.

For instance, if you are considering that refusing plans with friends often is a problem that is contributing towards your disconnect from them, leading to increased loneliness, it would be prudent to delve into it further and understand it at a deeper level. You may need to ask additional questions like, 'What is it that prompts me to refuse these plans?' 'Is it something about me or about the others?' 'Am I getting too tired?' 'Are the days being suggested not suitable for me?' 'Is there something about the conversations that I dislike?' or 'Is there a past situation which has triggered me?'

Further, asking such questions leads to an accumulation of facts and information that is going to aid in the creation of a strategy to circumvent the challenges you face and move in the direction of a *workable solution*.

Break It Down into Smaller Bits

Processing the whole situation may be difficult. You may feel almost paralysed to take that step. It is natural for you to feel anxious and overwhelmed. There is a lot of inertia you need to break through, and agony that must be resolved, before you are able to move forward. Doing something for the first time and doing it differently are contributing factors to your inertia. When the problem appears to be big, the solution too can feel like immense work, putting you under a lot of pressure.

A critical element that would aid this process is breaking

down that large chunk in front of you into multiple smaller bits. It makes the problem more manageable and it ceases to feel like such a big problem. Your journey to success requires that you take one step at a time and every little step that you do take moves you one step closer to resolving the problem. The cumulative effect of all these multiple steps will take you to the larger solution you seek.

In the situation we considered above with your friends when you asked yourself all those questions, you got a wealth of information you needed to place it all in a hierarchy and start with the least difficult step first. If you identified the day that is chosen as a part of the problem, then you start by suggesting an alternate day to your friends. You share with them the reason why that particular day of the week is especially difficult for you and in its place also provide a couple of solutions by suggesting two alternatives at least. You then move to the next part of the problem which could be, 'I feel lazy after work and once I am home, I find it difficult to motivate myself to get ready and step out again.' Identifying this as a problem, you can solve it by determining that you would suggest a time to meet which doesn't give you the time to first go home and instead you can go straight from work and meet your friends. You can also put a rule in place that for every invite you refuse, you would ensure you do not refuse the next.

In this manner, bit by bit, piece by piece, you take steps to move closer to solving this problem which has been one aspect contributing to the loneliness you feel.

Find Inspiration in People

Much of what you can do can come from your own understanding. The way you approach the situation and the solutions you see are largely a function of what you have had exposure to and, in part, to your own creativity. The way your mind sees things has got a lot to do with how you believe they can be worked through and resolved. However, there is another method that can act as a solid adjunct to your process.

Finding inspiration in others can have significant benefits, especially in situations where you feel like you're running into a wall and cannot find an outlet. Looking at how others may work through similar situations can give your thought process a new lease of life, a direction and a purpose. Inspiration doesn't always come on its own. You can't keep waiting to turn the corner and bump into it at some point.

Inspiration can be found in those around you who share your passions and with whom you have a common vision for life. It comes when you ask them questions, listen to their stories and understand their experiences. Through an authentic engagement with them, you can find knowledge that otherwise would remain hidden. In mutually sharing and discussing—looking at both the good and the bad, the successes and the failures—you can find new perspectives.

Learning, and Not Results

To start with, the focus needs to be on learning. The results need to consciously and actively be placed on the side. It isn't that the outcomes aren't important. To be able to discern in depth what affects the outputs most, it is important to stay steadfastly oriented towards looking at and evaluating the process. Focusing on it facilitates the development of an understanding of what affects the outputs, in what manner and by how much. Your understanding is likely to expand as the factors you thought were important initially may get supplemented by others you identify as being critical now.

Focusing on understanding these elements and utilizing your understanding to inform the acquisition of skills, the development of competence and mastery of situations, are far more helpful in the long run. It boosts confidence and sustains motivation when you see the results shift as you acquire diverse skills instead of focusing solely on the end product. It allows the application of these skills across different domains, leading to a continually improving model of functioning.

So don't give up on your goals if you don't see the results emerge immediately. Keep pruning the ineffective elements in your process and you would discover that you are inching closer to your goal. You feel in charge, more in control, happier with the steady progress and not disappointed that the results have not emerged yet.

Slow and Steady Wins the Race

Action increases the likelihood of you engaging in more action. Taking slow, steady steps towards reaching your goals is important. In pushing for too much or in moving too fast you can stumble, fall and lose your confidence. Keep making incremental changes that build upon a strong foundation and facilitate the process of a solid shift that leads to more durable changes in the long run. In attempting to make the big leap you can end up falling. So beware of these pitfalls and work on improving and changing one piece at a time.

14

BUILDING PSYCHOLOGICAL FLEXIBILITY

Important principles may, and must, be inflexible.

—Abraham Lincoln

Nothing in the world is more flexible and yielding than water. Yet when it attacks the firm and the strong, none can withstand it, because they have no way to change it. So the flexible overcome the adamant, the yielding overcome the forceful. Everyone knows this, but no one can do it.

—Lao Tzu

Emotional agility is about loosening up, calming down and living with more intention. It's about choosing how you'll respond to your emotional warning system.

—Susan David

As you sit waiting to be called in for your review, you find yourself wondering about how the feedback would be this time round. The previous few times your seniors had spoken to you, they had highlighted how you need to consider being more flexible in your approach.

This whole concept has been evading you. Not just in your professional space but even with your partner, you find that you are increasingly being reminded that you need to be flexible—enjoy the moment. But what you really keep feeling is a sense of being more and more out of control. The situations around you, the actions of those others who surround you, keep leaving you feeling perplexed. It is difficult to be *flexible*! It is difficult to just let things be (that's the meaning you have inferred when you are repeatedly told to be flexible).

THE UPSIDE OF BEING FLEXIBLE

Situations do not remain in our control. New variables can impinge upon us. The circumstances can vary widely. New information can come our way which can challenge our pre-existing ways of responding to them. All these can leave us feeling perplexed and uncertain. They create a challenge to determine a new way of responding. Or perhaps you need to find a way to adapt the existing way of being and responding.

If you think that you can rigidly adhere to your own notions of how things need to be, then you are setting yourself up for failure. When it comes to combatting the loneliness you experience, having a measure of flexibility in your thinking and approach is a must. You must adhere to your core values and you do not need to become a different person, so to say. However, there does need to be an ability to be variable in being able to work through these stresses you've identified that exacerbate the loneliness you experience.

In being flexible, holding on to your thoughts and feelings

more lightly, you give yourself the opportunity to be able to act in accordance with your goals and values. Instead of having to respond to thoughts and emotions that are fleeting and transitory, you allow yourself the opportunity to disengage and step back and respond in a way that is of value to you. You can adapt to the fluctuating situations that surround you, while you reconfigure the mental resources that you need to bring together to respond to the situation. You give yourself the opportunity to shift your perspective and not get stuck to a pattern of thinking, feeling or responding.

Even as the environmental context changes and goes through its own transitions, you afford yourself the option to make a choice and find the balance that works for you in managing your desires, needs and the demands placed upon you by life domains. So you don't need to suppress your inner experiences. Instead, you make a mindful choice.

Blocking Out Is Not an Option

The emotions and thoughts that come to your mind cannot be blocked out. There may be times when you can distract yourself from indulging in them. But preventing their occurrence is usually not in your control. A larger problem can ensue in trying to run away from the thoughts or feelings you are having. It would take you away from your goals and the efforts you know you need to make to achieve the outcomes you desire.

It is, instead, far more crucial to find a way to stay connected to your experiences but, at the same time, not getting rattled by them. Being able to remain aware of their presence and not get too impacted by them holds the key. Freeing up your internal resources to stay committed to the actions you need to engage in is going to be critical to the success of this approach.

You do this is by becoming more observant. You start by learning to acknowledge what goes on within you. That is the first step, as we had discussed. You build upon it by learning to notice them and deriving the information that is most useful for you. If you are getting swept up in them, losing your bearings and feeling overwhelmed, then you must take a step back, take a few deep breaths and try to notice your environment and find the label for what you are experiencing. Determine the patterns that you engage in so you can find a way to modify them. And, keep pushing yourself to take actions that are going to be more in accordance with the values you wish to reflect over the long run.

Find the Courage

In deciding to inculcate this approach, you should also be willing to be courageous. It takes courage to face your own thoughts and emotions. It can sound easy, but is in fact a difficult aspect to put into practice. The natural tendency for most people is to want to run away from, hide and avoid experiences which are difficult. You may crave for a life that is easy, flows smoothly and is largely unaffected by strong thoughts, emotions or difficult situations that require you to alter your approach too much.

Despite what you wish, at some stage or the other, you are likely to come across difficult circumstances in which your traditional way of approaching may not lead to desirable results. Being flexible in your thoughts and actions then becomes challenging. It means allowing you to be vulnerable to try out something new and different. It means allowing you to be vulnerable to, perhaps, do nothing but just let your thoughts and feelings be. This can be paradoxical and contradictory to what your natural inclination is.

So stop overemphasizing positive thinking or letting go. Instead, lay emphasis on being willing to face your thoughts and emotions. Face the situations you find yourself in. Be open to try out this new approach. Remember, thoughts and emotions are just what they are—they do not reflect an alternate reality and they cannot direct actions without your choosing to do something. So see yourself as a person who is filled with numerous possibilities and is not a one-trick pony.

Follow the Path Less Travelled

It is naturally easy to look at a situation and feel drawn towards the typical way of responding. You may feel tempted to consider what another person might do if they found themselves in the same scenario. This takes away your creativity in finding a solution that is unique to you and will give you the results that you are seeking.

Despite how difficult it may seem, and how hard you may feel it is to apply or the resistance, you feel, you may face in altering your way of viewing and responding, you must be willing to take that risk. People around you will be adaptable. They will also respond to your altered ways of responding. They may need some time to understand and adapt but, despite their initial resistance or even wariness, they are likely to undergo their own transitions.

To find your happiness and an approach that is working for you, your willingness and will to make these changes and travel the path less travelled will hold the key. You will falter in your approach and you may find yourself reverting to old ways of viewing and responding to situations. But do not be too quick to judge yourself. This is natural. As, in developing a new approach, the old will certainly throw in some resistance at you. It will cause an interference, yet, you will be able to keep reverting to your new approach if you consciously remind yourself about the need to do so.

The Goodness of Change

You may fear change. You may wonder about your own ability to adapt and you may reminisce about the comfort of things operating in a steady manner. Yet, there is immense goodness in change, which is facilitated by your willingness to be adaptive and flexible, in your thoughts, feelings and actions.

Change brings with it opportunity. It gives you the option to be creative. It lets you experiment and find something new, something more desirable. Till you don't try out and test out new options you will never know what more there can be and whether it can be something better than what you already have. In being stretched and pushed to extend yourself outside of your comfort zone, challenging your assumptions, mindset and ways of responding, you can find a new approach that will get you to your goals.

The process of discovery is not restricted to outside you. You will learn far more about your own self in embracing change and being flexible.

This Too Shall Pass

As you identify the unique challenges you face and you alter your approach, inculcating psychological flexibility and strive towards being agile, you will encounter some difficulty. It can create a feeling of being fragile as you negotiate your way through the different challenges that come your way. Combatting this loneliness, you must keep in mind that by staying committed to taking actions based on your core values and not allowing transitory thoughts and feelings to take you away from your course of action, you will find your desired goal. Being patient is important, as is staying truly committed to yourself and to your decided course of action. Give yourself adequate time to be able to implement what you have in mind.

15

BRING IN WORK-LIFE BALANCE

Don't confuse having a career with having a life.

—Hillary Rodham Clinton

Work is a rubber ball. If you drop it, it will bounce back. The other four balls—family, health, friends, integrity—are made of glass. If you drop one of these, it will be irrevocably scuffed, nicked, perhaps even shattered.

—Gary Keller

There's no such thing as work-life balance. There are work-life choices, and you make them, and they have consequences.

—Jack Welch

As you sit listening to your friend talk about all that he has been doing, you wonder about where you lost sight of all the other things you used to insist were important in your life—things that you had pledged would always be present. Somewhere, in doing your work and handling your responsibilities, you feel like you have lost sight of those *other things* which were so important to you. You try to think of when it all happened but your mind struggles to point towards that one instance that you can label as the turning point in your life. You feel it was perhaps an amalgamation of things. Your mind knows that it was a slow, subtle shift that kept happening and you just did not realize when that magic term, *work-life balance,* went missing for you.

Knowing What Is Important

The decisive element in resolving the issues you have identified as the cause of your loneliness is figuring out what is important. As you proceed through the different phases and stages of your life, there is a certain amount of automaticity associated with it. In a fairly clinical manner, you move from one thing to the next and keep shifting your values and goals without necessarily making a conscious choice and carefully thinking through, 'Is this really what I want?'

These decisions and the trajectory you follow is predetermined on the basis of what you had heard and known while growing up—the expected ways of being and doing things. Your mind does not naturally gravitate towards thinking and asking the question, 'What would I have done had I not known this is the supposed natural next step?' Such questions, in fact, are unlikely to surface in your mind. It is easier to follow the herd and keep nudging yourself towards that natural, socially determined next step.

In this process, you also forget to answer for yourself, 'What holds importance for me?' It becomes a given that you would not be raising questions and would follow suit with what the expectations are. Usually, in today's times, these are usually about finishing school and then college, going to one of the A-listed universities through which you can get the best placement and, as a result, the best remuneration for the work you would be doing. Once you have that job in hand and everyone around you affirms that you are now financially stable, you take the step towards settling down with a partner—of your own choice or with someone you are introduced to by family or friends. After this is done, you once again shift focus to the workplace. After all, you must ensure there is substantial, periodic growth in your roles and positions to be able to provide for and keep supporting yourself and your family.

In doing all this, it is likely that you forget about the other side—the one that looks at your family, for whom you want to work, and yourself, whose ambitions you wish to satisfy. Unconsciously, your choices keep taking you away from a lot of what you had desired in your younger years—music, games, dance, art, reading, relaxing. Many of these can begin to feel like chores and often, a lot of them even go missing from the list of things you would absolutely love to do.

It Is Not Selfish

If and when you do begin to think of the things you would have liked to incorporate in your routines, your mind can pull you back and you may wonder, 'Am I being selfish? Should I not prioritize the needs of my family?' Your mind can play tricks and make you feel as though the choice you are making would lead to you being seen as irresponsible or even awful. Even as you make some choices to include the things you like, you may feel the pressure to not make it too much and to tread with great caution, lest you forget about what is important for the family.

Even as you grew up you heard it being reinforced that every person has a role and it comes with its own responsibilities. You cannot run away from these and, in fact, must proactively work to ensure that none of these get missed or ignored. But what was not mentioned along this route you were perhaps encouraged to take was that to be a giver and a doer, you also need to be in a position mentally, emotionally and physically to contribute to another's life or even towards your own work.

Giving and doing are activities that can deplete our energy. To restore your enery reserves to continuously keep striving to engage and stay involved, you need to ensure that your needs are being met. Making time to find a balance and integrating the things you like becomes a necessity. To feel relaxed, rejuvenated and ready to take on the challenges of each day, you need to be able to direct some focus towards your own self as well, and this is most certainly not being selfish.

Balance Comes With Drawing Boundaries

Maintaining a balance is possible only if you are willing to draw boundaries. Without boundaries, both around work as well as your relationships, you will struggle to find the mechanisms to take care of yourself. People around you will always take their cues from you. So if you want to find the time and space to be able to do things for yourself and strike that right balance for yourself, you need to provide the right cues.

The responsibility of drawing that line, which defines for everyone your limits, rests with you. In defining your relationships and the amount they can stretch you and push you, you empower yourself and provide yourself with a feeling of control. It allows you to protect yourself from feeling depleted at the end of the day or week. You find your own ways of recharging yourself as well.

These boundaries can be put in place by first identifying your own limits, both at work as well as in your personal relationships. Defining and clearly specifying these, without being aggressive or agitated, is important and this would be possible if you attempt to maintain these from an early stage in your relationships. You need to pay attention to the feelings that are evoked within you to be able to communicate to others what you need and why drawing that boundary is important to you.

Bend Gently

Rigidity in any form or format can be detrimental. Bringing in the flexibility we spoke of previously, even in the scenarios that pertain to your work-life balance, is rather critical. You may, at times, need to reconsider and reassess the boundaries you are drawing for those around you and even at work. This should not result in you being a complete pushover, willing to entirely alter what you feel you need for yourself. There must be a process of bending gently, slowly, yet surely, to ensure that you are not left feeling completely consumed and depleted by your mental, emotional, psychological and physical engagements.

This process of altering and bending must occur in a way that it does not lead to feelings of resentment or anger in your relationship with others. It should also not cause you to despise your workplace because that would automatically take away from your productivity. If the negative feelings towards doing what you are doing and the amount you are engaging in it are increasing, then it would mean that you need to focus on the process of drawing the right boundaries.

Communication Is Necessary

In the face of such situations where you are feeling tired and exhausted, it is possible that your mind harbours various thoughts. These could be: 'I wish others around me would just understand,' 'I just need some peace and quiet' or 'Why won't people let me be and let me do my own thing?' You start having this expectation that in some magical manner, people around you—be it in your personal spaces or your workplace—will know when to approach you and when to leave you alone.

No one around you has the ability or the inclination to read your mind. Every individual is likely to be coping with their own set of things that are difficult for them. In such a scenario, you alone can be the one who can share and communicate with clarity and precision what you are feeling, thinking and what you may need from them.

Clarity in your communication is going to be rather important in ensuring that your life moves forward in a direction that appeals to you. There will be times when, despite your communication, things may not alter and shift. But these situations are going to be lesser than what they would be if you chose to not communicate your needs.

There Will be Pushback

It is not that all will go smoothly from the moment you set your boundaries and begin to incorporate the things that you like and indulge in activities you want to. There is certainly going to be some pushback. This will happen at all fronts. Resistance from other sources is going to be a natural response to the changes you are attempting to bring into effect.

This is, in fact, indicative of the need to keep working towards putting these boundaries in place. The resistance will eventually wear away and people and systems around you will fall into a new, albeit different rhythm. Patience is a must in this scenario. There will also be a lot of back and forth in terms of negotiating around the boundaries that you are attempting to set. You would need to maintain your persistence and insist upon finding that time for yourself and for the things that you would desire to include.

You Are Worthy

In these situations, you can begin to question your need and feel like you are over-stretching, judging the situations you are in too harshly and being unreasonable in demanding the balance that you are seeking. You must recognize that you are worthy and deserve to find that balance for your well-being and to ensure the quality of your work as well as your relationships. The sustenance of all that you are working towards is feasible only if you recognize the need to focus on you and don't challenge yourself about it.

16

INDULGE AND PRIORITIZE YOURSELF

I will not let anyone walk through my mind with their dirty feet.

—Mahatma Gandhi

By taking care of myself I have so much more to offer the world than I do when I am running on empty.

—Ali Washington

If you do not take control over your time and your life, other people will gobble it up. If you don't prioritize yourself, you constantly start falling lower and lower on your list.

—Michelle Obama

As you lie in bed, reading your book, your mind wanders off towards thoughts of how you wish you had more control over parts of your life. You think of the narratives of others around you who claim that they have been doing what they love, pursuing their passions and hobbies, without a worry in the world. Even as your mind recognizes the improbability of a completely happy scenario in those other people's lives, you still feel drawn to consider the possibility of it. You find yourself introspecting, 'What would I do if I had these options?' The answers span many areas. You recognize that there are unlimited options you could consider. But it isn't that easy to prioritize yourself and to indulge in something that your heart and mind desire when each day you are reminded of the realities of your existence and the roles and responsibilities you need to fulfil.

A Healthier, Happier You

Growing up, you are taught and encouraged to remember how being selfless and putting the needs of others above your own is very important. In doing this, however, you can discover that you are pushing yourself to the limit, exceeding your capacity to keep doing and giving. You may end up being in a space where, even as you recognize that you are beginning to struggle, you may hesitate to share this knowledge with those who surround you.

Socrates said, 'Care for oneself and know oneself'. In order to be centred, comfortable, happy and content, you must strive to prioritize yourself—over others, over work. You can find that person you seek if you decide to take steps towards indulging yourself a little bit. It does not come with simply forgetting and letting go of everyone and everything else. But it does necessitate a slight readjustment and realignment of the way in which you see things and in which you operate across the different domains of your life.

You will find a healthier and happier you if you reflect upon your needs and take the time to respond to what you are feeling and thinking. Often, these can get ignored and shoved into the back-burner. They become less important in the midst of the plethora of things that appear at your doorstep daily. There are many pulls and pushes on a daily basis towards everything else that is not about you per se. But caring for others is possible only if you learn how to balance it with caring for yourself.

Maintaining a sense of regard for yourself, being compassionate and indulging in self-care, are important elements which many of us can forget in the rat race of living a *good life*. This good life, which is envisaged, does not necessarily lead to your happiness as it may take you away from the very things you love and would want to indulge in if you were to choose to prioritize yourself a little bit.

Don't Lose Yourself

In the constant, persistent go-go-go and do-do-do of everyday living, you can easily forget about yourself. You may end up finding yourself swiftly moving from one thing to the next, making everything a priority except for your own self and the things that you like and would love to do and indulge in. As you keep placing weight on what the needs of your parents are or your children are or what your boss wants, you actively detract from anything that would relate to what your needs are.

In doing these daily tasks, you begin to derive your sense of worthiness from all that you managed to do for everyone else and in the context of the things that you did for others. Your own self and its needs do not occupy centre stage and you keep losing a part of you. You don't even take a breath to pause and evaluate what this doing and going and achieving is doing for you, and the meaning and value that it holds for you. Your measure of its necessity gets based upon the response you keep receiving from others that reinforces their strong need for all you are doing for them.

You may not even realize it, but a harsh inner voice may find a place within yourself which, perhaps, berates you for placing yourself in a position where you want to do things for yourself. It becomes insistent on deriving your sense of goodness from that which is valued by others around you and which satisfies their needs and desires.

Saying 'No'

Refusing another is always difficult. This is especially so when this other is someone you cherish and value. Even when it relates to work, your need to ensure you are above and beyond everyone else and do things that will place you at the helm of things, prevents you from being able to refuse and you perhaps find yourself assuming more responsibilities, despite feeling stressed and strained by what you already do.

Saying 'no' is not something you may have been taught. In fact, growing up, you would have been encouraged to indulge in others' requests and try and see if you could find a way of satisfying their needs. Your family, perhaps, displayed the same behaviour and you may not have realized how strong an influence that would have had on shaping your responses. Your inability to refuse someone was learnt not just through direct instruction but also through absorbing a lot of what your family displayed.

Today, at this juncture of life, where you assess and evaluate where you are at and how you lead your life, it is important to recognize the important role that learning to say 'no' can play in your life. It would help you draw the right boundaries and also reinforce your need to have your own agency in determining what you do and what you don't.

None of this would happen overnight. It would require practice. You may need to start by learning to first defer requests and find a way to negotiate what is being demanded with what you can realistically supply and support. At times, you would need to be able to delegate and then finally move towards saying 'no' to what you know is not feasible and realistically possible for you.

Practise Self-Compassion

The problem in continually doing things for others around you is that you run the risk of forgetting to feel for and about your own self. You miss out on being kind to yourself. You push yourself and relentlessly expect that you will bear more burdens and shoulder more responsibilities. You refuse to recognize when you are getting overstretched and when you absolutely cannot manage anymore.

This leads to a tendency towards being overly self-critical and having least patience with yourself, which eventually impacts your moods and alters the way you think. A negative approach can certainly wiggle its way into your mindset and you would not even realize that this process has begun to impact you. You may wonder why you need to consider being self-compassionate. The reason lies in the fact that in being kind to yourself, you can better look at your mistakes and take remedial actions rather than being excessively harsh with your own self.

This self-compassion involves recognizing and accepting the thoughts and feelings you have, taking a non-judgmental stance towards them and being comfortable with not having full control over them. Recognizing your struggles and being comfortable with their presence would lead you to being able to adopt a proactive problem-solving approach and allow you to find your happiness and contentment.

Six Mantras for Prioritizing Yourself

Here are a few things which you should keep in mind in order to keep prioritizing yourself as an important aspect of your functioning.

- Make a steady, consistent effort to find time daily to pause and reflect on what you feel and what you want to achieve. Having this approach can enable you to find your contentment on a daily basis and keep refreshing in your mind all that you would like to do for yourself.
- Focus on the path you take, instead of looking at the outcomes. The process and approach have greater value. Outcomes relate to so much more that can be outside of your control. As you focus on the process,

you feel relaxed with what you are doing and how much you are doing.
- Find the steps that work for you. Do things that you need to do but in a way that works for you. Remember, you do not need to follow a specific approach that others may adopt. Your own unique methodology can be revelatory in itself and give you the success that you desire.
- Find the time for the things you love. There is no fixed frequency that you must follow but ensuring that you do indulge in the activities that you love regularly is important.
- Be willing to step back and let others take the lead. Even as you delegate or say 'no' to things, you will not end up losing out on your progress. There will always be more opportunities and, if you do balance things for yourself, you will find enhanced capacity for creativity, problem-solving and decision-making.
- Comfortably seek support from friends and family. Reach out to them if you struggle to do something. Don't hesitate to talk if you need to solicit their help.

Evade Perfection

In working towards prioritizing yourself, let go of your need to have a perfect approach. Making mistakes must be permissible. Learning is the key here. Make your errors, take feedback and be willing to experiment. As you keep modifying things and swapping the pieces around, you will reach that ultimate balanced state that would most suit your needs and your approach. Don't stop just because you are struggling at first. Keep working ahead and believe that you would surely reach the right solution for yourself!

17

LOOK FOR SOLUTIONS

One can choose to go back toward safety or forward toward growth. Growth must be chosen again and again; fear must be overcome again and again.

—Abraham Maslow

Look for the solutions, instead of being difficult; be more thoughtful, instead of allowing anger to burn you out. Look at things from a different perspective, embrace change, look out for opportunities and you will feel much more in control.

—Steve Backley

We must look within ourselves, become responsible and provide fresh solutions if we ever want to do more than complain, or make excuses.

—Nelson Mandela

You have been having a difficult time in your relationship with your friend. In the last three months that you have met with each other, you have a felt a strain in the conversations. You have noticed that she reacts in an uncharacteristically harsh manner each time you make a suggestion. After meeting your friend the last few times, you spoke about it with your sibling. In every instance that you narrated, your sibling attempted to provide a solution. But you recognized that you kept rejecting each suggestion. It was as though your mind was just refusing to budge from the problem you were finding yourself in. You were seeking validation for how you were feeling, and reinforcement that you had not made a mistake. You were left feeling as though you just did not want to look for, and move in the direction of, a solution. You were finding yourself stuck to the problem and that was riling you up from inside.

The Search

The problem of being in a problem state is that there is process you need to indulge in that involves searching for a much-needed viable solution. This search is for a way to reduce the distance between where you are and where you want to get to. You would have engaged in this process of searching a number of times and you must have realized that it's easy to define a number of problems. This makes the decision-making process of how to get to the end point easier. But, there is a much larger corresponding number of problems that are rather hard to specify. Fleshing out their precise details can be challenging, and as a result, getting to the goal that is defined by them can seem impossible.

You can end up finding yourself, far more often, in a rather ill-defined problem state in your life as you navigate through diverse situations. It is not just the path towards resolving that problem which may be difficult to map out. In fact, it is also possible that it is complicated to even attempt to define how much of the problem exists, or how much of movement is required on your part to solve it.

You will also recognize that in most situations, there is no one best way of resolving a problem. The first thought or solution that pops up in your mind may not always be the best one. You may need to push your mind to keep the search engine running so that it can come up with an array of solutions. This, in turn, will enable you to choose the one that is most applicable and would provide you with the best results in the given scenario. This whole process is arduous and can feel burdensome. It is exhausting and the thought of it can make you feel drained.

When you consider this problem of loneliness that you are attempting to confront and resolve, the situation is no different. You may believe that fixing one variable may give you the desired result. But you may end up discovering that you need to think more and search more, necessarily requiring you to move far more pieces around than what you had originally bargained for. In pushing yourself to consider diverse aspects and look at the problem from varying vantage points, you will find yourself discovering parts to the solution that may have otherwise evaded you.

The Many Steps to Reaching a Solution

Looking for the solution starts with knowing and understanding the problem. To know a problem, you need to be aware of the varying aspects related to it. You must find answers to the questions—what, why and how—when you are attempting to know what exactly the problem is. By asking these questions, you will discover numerous elements about the problem which may not be easily apparent or observable otherwise.

When you understand the problem, you need to take steps that help you to formulate a strategy. It must be informed by as much information as is possibly available with you. To do so, you must make yourself aware of what it is that you do know about the problem and what are the pieces of information that you do not have available with you. This ensures that the solution you are implementing can likely be the best possible one. However, a final judgment or decision about its effectiveness can only be made once you have implemented it.

This means that you would need to keep reviewing the solution you have implemented and be ready to make adjustments and accommodations to your original thought process. Keeping a vigil on the outcomes is necessary to ensure that your proposed solution does not run into a substantial roadblock. Even if it does, there has to be willingness and wilfulness to keep persisting with this cycle of moving from problem to strategy to testing the strategy and evaluating the outcomes and then adjusting and fine-tuning based on the results that you obtain.

There Will Be Many Emotions

The biggest source of difficulty in problem scenarios will arise from the plethora of emotions that you experience, even as you work towards finding a solution for them. These emotions will be difficult to isolate, understand and manage. In fact, you may also realize that you find it a perplexing task to even identify the exact emotion you are feeling in a situation of substantial hardship.

In most situations, you will recognize that you experience a range of conflicting emotions and a singular emotional experience is certainly not the norm. For instance, when you have a challenge at your workplace in understanding a task and implementing the strategy that has been suggested to you, you might experience irritability, anger, frustration, despair, helplessness, sadness and perhaps even excitement and nervousness. This range of emotions carries the potential of leaving you with a feeling of confusion. Growing up, you are not taught that in most situations, this is what your emotional experience is likely to be. Instead, we usually think about our emotional states as being singularly toned. This is far removed from the reality of what emotional experiences are like in reality.

Accepting that emotions are going to occupy a significant space is important. Appreciating that they will have a strong role to play is even more critical. It would enhance your ability to be able to step away from a situation as soon as you find yourself reeling under its influence and impact.

Don't Let Habit Overtake

Being in a comfort zone makes everything easy. This comfort zone arises out of a sense of habit. But getting stuck in this comfort zone can be detrimental to your own growth and happiness. Albeit the process of moving out of your comfort zone by breaking your habit can be taxing; it takes energy to push yourself to make a move. You may link it to a lack of motivation and believe that you are stuck because you lack the drive to change things. However, this is not likely to be the case.

Low motivation or drive can be a reason. But it is certainly not the only reason. In most situations, the reason is that we find making changes an arduous task. It is easy to let the habit overtake you and keep you stuck behind it. It can behave like that annoying car ahead of you which refuses to follow the speed limit and keeps coming in front of your car each time you try to overtake it.

Moving towards your potential accords you happiness. This potential needs to be realized even in the context of the loneliness you experience. It is possible to stretch yourself a little and find new avenues to break free from the repetitive cycle you are stuck in. Taking one small step at a time is going to be the key. As long as there is movement, there will be a feeling of progress. The end goal needs to be in sight but so do the smaller, more realizable steps.

Not everyone discovers the most satisfying way of living their lives at an early stage. This means everyone does not have the mechanisms in place that allow them to feel like they are realizing the true potential of their selves in the different contexts of their lives. Seeing this as a journey is important. Being willing to keep the process of discovery as an important goal for yourself will be helpful in ensuring you do not stay stuck to your habits.

Build the Skills

Be open and willing to build the requisite skills that are needed in the problem scenario you are facing. When it concerns loneliness, it is possible that you may struggle with aspects of time management, prioritizing, balancing your work with other aspects of your life, communication-related skills, to name a few. Identify the areas that are causing you concern and be committed to working on those.

Making a concerted, dedicated, determined effort to modify and build your skills is an important element which can get ignored. Particularly, if you allow yourself to be preoccupied with the emotions that you are experiencing in the given scenario. You need to consciously look at these skills, which you need to build, within the context of their constituting elements. Looking at a big skill that you feel is missing might trigger self-defeating thoughts. So make an effort to break it up into smaller bits and keep taking slow but steady steps towards implementing them.

Get the Right Support in Place

Resolving any problematic state can be stressful. Having your sources of support in place is necessary so you don't falter and fumble. You need to ensure that you keep sharing and discussing the challenges you are facing with a friend or a family member or even an expert so that you can keep steering yourself in the right direction. A gentle prodding is always helpful. At the same time, you can gather the perspectives of your support system to ensure you are, in fact, moving along in the right direction and to the right place.

Besides providing you with a buffer and a sounding board, the presence of your support system will also ensure that you get a mental break from the overwhelming thoughts and emotions that can get triggered in such a situation. Having the option of people around you who can help you work through these would be beneficial in the long run. Their presence and becoming a part of the solution would also ensure that it strengthens the relationships you have with each other. This, too, is crucial for your well-being and your happiness.

Not Everything Can Be Solved

Despite your best efforts, there will always be some situations that may still not have a solution. Accepting this reality is essential for you to cope with the problems you find surrounding you. It is imperative that you push towards looking at the hard work and efforts you are putting in, in your attempt to search for a solution. Your perseverance and will to keep working towards resolving problems is a far more valuable skill. Refrain from passing judgments on yourself on the basis of the number of situations or problems you manage to solve. Instead, stay focused on the process you adopted.

18

HOLD YOUR FEELINGS IN BALANCE

Feelings, emotions—they are neither right nor wrong. They cannot be assigned a value. Feelings 'are'. By labelling a feeling wrong, you force yourself to ignore that feeling. And what you most need is to feel it, let it burn through you, then get on with life.

—Karen Marie Moning

Nothing can bring you peace but yourself.

—Ralph Waldo Emerson

You should never make a permanent decision based on a temporary feeling.

—Justin Bariso

You're sitting at a table in the restaurant waiting for your friend to arrive. There is a couple sitting at the adjoining table, talking animatedly, their voices getting successively louder as they attempt to make their points. You can't help but overhear the conversation and to your mind it seems fairly trivial—the girl got talking to a friend and got late in reaching the restaurant. You can see the emotions building up, the girl's eyes welling up, the boy getting agitated. The more they talk, the more their disagreement appears to increase. They struggle to keep their emotions in check. It sounds like this is not the first time they are fighting on a similar issue. They keep referring back to other instances, each of them stuck to their own version and experience of the situation. Not being able to listen to each other, they seem driven by their emotional experience of the time. It reminds you of the many times you have been in a similar space—stuck to your version, your emotions, not being able to create the space in your mind at the time to listen to the other, feeling overwhelmed, feeling stuck and just wanting to escape but not knowing how to and what to do with what you were feeling at the time.

Feelings 'Are'

Your feelings are and can be many things and yet they can be just that—words that are supposed to make you be a certain way. The meaning you attribute to the feelings you experience determines, to a large extent, what your actions and responses are within situations. You may be tempted to want to attribute much meaning to them, delve into them and allow yourself to respond on their basis. But the reality is that feelings are states that just happen. They arise unbidden. They come without your conscious decision. They emerge spontaneously. They can surprise and shock you.

They can become the reasons why you act a certain way. When that happens, you may not make the best decision in that situation. In fact, if it felt good or bad and you decided to do or not do something, the resulting outcome may not necessarily be the desired one. For instance, it may feel good to just lie in bed and not make the effort of dragging yourself out, getting ready and going to meet your friends. But after you do respond to and prioritize that feeling, you find that you are unhappy. You are missing out on all the fun and now you feel morose and life looks desolate and moribund.

So it may seem like what you do need to do is not prioritize what feels right. Instead, in its place, it is far more important to look at doing things in a manner that is, in fact, good or better or right for your life. But doing this is not easy. It is far easier to act on the basis of what you feel and respond to situations in the light of the strongest feeling that is emerging for you at the time. And this has the potential to make you respond impulsively, not necessarily take into account the full situation or what your reaction will lead to in terms of its impact on other people.

It is then imperative that you understand a few things about your feelings. They are transitory and they pass. They do not always stay fixed and they are likely to get modified as your experiences change. Your feelings are often dictated by your past experiences and by the prevailing thought process that you have been indulging in. This can make them inaccurate at times and thus, it is important to be wary of reacting too soon and too strongly on their basis. Your feelings are within you and are known only to you. They are not evident to anyone else. So if you want people to respond to what you are feeling, you will need to be willing to express them.

Don't Let Feelings Overwhelm You

When you face challenges, you cannot allow the emotions emerging within you to overwhelm you. You may find this to be a difficult task and it can require immense effort. A first step in being able to adopt this approach would necessitate that you accurately understand and label the emotion that you are experiencing in the given situation. So you need to look towards building your emotional vocabulary, keeping in mind that you may experience numerous emotions in any situation.

These emotions typically arise due to the thoughts being generated within your mind. Let's take the example of the situation we looked at in the previous chapter where you are perhaps struggling to understand a task and implement the strategy that was being suggested to you. One of the emotions you were experiencing was anger. As you were being repeatedly explained the task and the strategy that you need to implement, the person doing the explaining was not able to understand the exact issue you had a difficulty in understanding. This was prompting him to approach you in a patronizing tone that you were inferring as, 'This person thinks I am stupid'. This thought was making you angry and the more he was continuing to use the same tone, the more you could feel your anger rising, and you had to make extra efforts to ensure that you did not react aggressively. So you chose to stay quiet, thinking, 'I'll figure it out myself'. However, that made you even more angry because it was triggering a previously held belief that, 'Every time I am in a good space at work something like this comes up to make it all bad. Now I will soon have to reassess my position here.'

Identifying this thought process, which relates to a belief system, is helpful in modulating the emotion as you can also identify the errors that exist in your thinking in such a circumstance. For example, the most prominent error here would firstly be to assume that something bad always happens when you are in a good space at your workplace. Secondly, jumping to the conclusion that you may need to reconsider your position at the workplace too involves an error in your thought process.

Identification of these errors allows for the opportunity to mediate the thought process in order to modulate the emotions you are experiencing in the situation. Adopting such an approach lets you ensure that you do not get overwhelmed by the emotions you may experience in a situation and you are able to manage them.

Controlling Is Not an Effective Strategy

Attempting to control the emotions you are feeling in a situation or the thoughts that are triggering them, is usually a futile strategy. In trying to control, you must make yourself more aware of their presence. This involves attributing more value to them and giving them increasing space in your cognitive processes. Being vigilant and on the lookout for their presence is distracting from other more important aspects that you must focus on instead.

Control is something that humans strive for, as dealing with ambiguity is often a formidable task. The paradox arises within the context of emotions, as the more you attempt to rein in the feelings, the more they spiral out of control. This occurs because you have feelings about how you are feeling and these become more prominent in your mind when you try to force them out. You can get reminded of how you tend to feel too much or feel too differently, leading to a process of judgment about yourself. When you see that you are feeling or reacting in ways that, in your view, others don't, they make you experience immense guilt. You don't like to be different and you don't want to be burdensome for others. Even as you want to stand out and be exceptional you don't want to be exceptional in how you feel—the average is more preferable in this regard.

Even if the emotions you feel are good, you don't want to become self-absorbed or be perceived as narcissistic. There is a pitfall on both sides of this dilemma about what to do with your feelings. Controlling them or attempting to do so is certainly not going to be the route according you the maximum benefits.

Reappraise the Meaning You Attach to Feelings

You may wonder, 'If the solution is not in attempting to control what I feel, what can I do instead?' Staying overwhelmed or thinking that you are a slave to your emotions is not going to allow you to move forward. As you work upon not getting overwhelmed by understanding your thinking and correcting the errors you might make in your thought process, you simultaneously need to work on the meanings you attribute to the feelings you do have.

Learning to hold your feelings lightly is a solution and

that happens by recognizing that your feelings may not always mean something substantial about the situation you are in. Focusing on reassessing and reappraising your feeling is important by asking yourself important questions like:

- Is what I am currently feeling related to a past experience?
- Am I attributing too much meaning to what I am feeling?
- Is there a different way to look at and process the situation?
- If someone else was in this scenario, what would I expect them to feel and be like?
- Do I really need to give importance to this feeling today?

When you ask yourself questions like these, you allow yourself to delink what you are feeling from the meaning you have been attributing all along. You can decide how much importance you are according this feeling that you are having and you can make a choice about whether to respond on the basis of this feeling or whether you should let it pass.

They Don't Say Anything About You

You may think that your feelings say a lot about who you are or the choices that you have made. How you feel across situations has nothing to do with how you are as a person. Your feelings do not and cannot define you. It is your actions—what you choose to do with your feelings—that will come to define you. What a feeling makes you think can be something that you control, but that is possible only if you build a psychological distance from them and view them as *just feelings*—nothing more, nothing less and not in your control, but certainly something that can be modified depending on the meaning you choose to attribute to them.

19

INVEST IN RELATIONSHIPS

No matter how brilliant your mind or strategy, if you're playing a solo game, you'll always lose out to a team.

—Reid Hoffman

The quality of our relationships determines the quality of our lives.

—Esther Perel

Real relationships are the product of time spent, which is why so many of us have so few of them.

—Craig D. Lounsbrough

Heading back from your workplace in the metro you see people chattering away—some with others next to them, others on the phone. Animated conversations surround you. Everyone seems to be eager to share and discuss something with the other person. Despite the fatigue evident in their expressions, they continue to engage with each other. It appears as though they have been waiting the whole day, gunning to share all that they did and saw, felt and expressed. You too crave for that feeling of belonging. You also want to have relationships that will make you feel valued and cherished. You know it needs some effort from you. To make it happen you would need to be willing to invest—your time, energy, effort, yourself—into the whole process.

The Magic of Shared Experiences

In running from pillar to post, getting tasks stricken off your to-do list, you end up investing tremendously in your work. Your experiences with others are relegated to the background and the magic that these shared interpersonal experiences can afford you is completely lost. It is lost even more so because your mind doesn't necessarily believe that there can be magic. In being stuck to the mundane and the routine you lose sight of the value that these moments can hold for you.

You need a reminder about the benefits you can accrue if you are willing to put aside some time to build these shared experiences. There is much goodness you can experience and happiness you can generate by choosing to invest in your relationships and creating the magic of shared experiences. Study after study has attested to the beneficial impact of simply focusing on building good relationships and the tremendous impact this can have upon every aspect of an individual's life.

Shared experiences lead to the creation of meaning and purpose between you and the other. This allows you to feel a greater sense of positivity about the kind of life you are leading and the engagements you have within the interpersonal sphere. In being able to share experiences with others, you find a space also for your emotions and thoughts, something that can certainly help you in building deeper connections. The more the shared experiences you accumulate, the better the quality of the relationship you have. These, thus, hold the key towards building more meaningful relationships in your life.

The enhanced feeling of connectedness builds on your mutual feeling of caring and being cared for. It also creates space for enhanced trust through the mutual exploration of the lives you lead, thus strengthening the overall relationship in the long run. The positive experiences you accumulate through having these meaningful relationships in your life allows you to maintain an overall positivity towards people and situations.

Small Investments Yield Big Dividends

It is natural to assume that building relationships and making the choice to invest in them may need you to be actively engaged in it most of the time. You may presume that you need to make rather large time commitments and emotional engagements to be able to build solid relationships that can last you a lifetime. However, that is certainly not the case. Small investments that you make in your relationship can yield large dividends.

You do not need to demarcate large proportions of time to meet someone or connect with them. A simple checking in can be helpful. It is more the regularity and consistency of making the investments in a relationship that is critical to its long-term sustenance. Your continued presence and involvement creates a secure foundation for the relationship. It engenders trust and security, facilitating greater levels of sharing by both the individuals within the relationship.

Big or grand gestures are misnomers and, in fact, can leave the other person feeling misled as you would struggle to maintain them. A one-off big gesture can create confusion in the mind of the other person and make them wonder about your commitment towards the relationship that you have with them. This does not mean that there should not be any grand gestures. Instead, these need to be interspersed with the smaller investments you need to make with far greater frequency and regularity.

Maintain the Intent

Make your intent known. Let the other person be aware of how you are thinking and what you are feeling. Sharing your plans and having a clear thought process about what you are seeking and how you see yourself being involved within the framework of the relationship you have is essential. This ensures that expectations are clarified and there are no misunderstandings that the other person may harbour. They are not likely to feel misled if they can see with great clarity what your intent is and if you can also ensure that they are maintained.

Vacillating in how you are within your relationship is unnerving and distressing for the other person. It also takes away their feeling of stability within their own life as your unpredictability can be perplexing. Having clarity about your own plans and schedules is always helpful and ensures that the other person too knows what and how much to expect from you.

However, it is important to also remember that there is another person and that any relationship is bidirectional. The other person too will come with their own set of needs and desires. They would also have their own goals which they would wish to achieve. These may not always be commensurate with what you have in mind and that could potentially create grounds for conflict.

Be Wary of Being Greedy

It is easy to fall into the trap of attaching enormous importance to, and only prioritizing, your own needs. There must be a balance in all you do and that is true of your relationships as well. Ensuring that you consciously create the space for the thoughts, feelings, expectations, needs, desires and experiences of the other person, who you are engaging with is equally important.

Getting swayed by your own thinking and immersing yourself in evaluating and assessing what is going on with you is likely to come naturally. But this is exactly what you must be wary of. You need to keep creating some space and actively step back. Ask yourself questions like: 'Am I getting too consumed by all that is going on with me?' 'Am I asking and being aware of the other person?' 'Am I only prioritizing my needs?'

By being overly focused on your own self and your own needs, you are actively reducing the time that can be accorded to the relationships you have. It is a choice that you make. But investing in your relationships means being cognisant of such choices that you do make and choosing to step away and act differently. Practising being generous in your relationships is a good place to start and that can happen only if you give yourself the time to ask, 'What does this other person need?' and 'How can I make the time to supply to that need?'

Perfectionism Can Lead to Your Undoing

In all that you do for your relationships, consciously steer away from attempting to be perfect. You will err and you will hurt others. The more important aspect is whether there is the intent to do so or not. The problem is not in erring or hurting but rather in not taking ownership of what has unfolded on account of your actions and the choices that you are making.

Taking responsibility and accepting ownership of all that you do are going to be important steps in letting the other people around you know the value they hold in your life. By being able to accept this aspect, you also acknowledge that you are ready to do something about it. But that doing something cannot be to move in the direction of being perfect in all your relationships.

Striving to be perfect can lead to your undoing and it means overburdening yourself and attempting to accomplish the impossible. The needs of others will be numerous and satisfying each would not be possible. So, perfection is not likely and striving for it will only be detrimental to your relationships because it will create resentment and anger as you experience immense fatigue in attempting to be that perfect person.

Self-Compassion Is Needed

As you strive to maintain and invest in your relationships, be prepared for setbacks. Allow yourself to experience failures. Strive for success, but be gentle with yourself. Find the ability to let yourself err. Do not pass judgments as you go through this process. There will be back and forth and you will find the balance. Be willing to give yourself some time to determine the right balance for yourself.

20

DIGITAL DETOX

Disconnecting from our technology to reconnect with ourselves is absolutely essential for wisdom.

—Arianna Huffington

I decided that the most subversive, revolutionary thing I could do was to show up for my life and not be ashamed.

—Anne Lamott

Sometimes you just have to unplug from everything to find yourself again.

—Robin Lee

You're sitting with a group of friends and the conversation hasn't been that engaging. You keep observing your hand sneak up towards your phone. The temptation to pick it up and get on to some social media platform can get quite overpowering. You like to keep browsing through something or the other. Even as you have been attempting to make a concerted effort to keep away from your phone, your eyes dart towards it. You keep feeling that you heard it beep—maybe you received a text and you should check. As you pick it up, you realize that it wasn't important but now that you do have your phone in your hand, you think, 'I can quickly scan through my apps. What's the harm?'

A Calmer You

Socrates said, 'To find yourself think for yourself.' In modern times, surrounded by gadgets, being constantly on the go, multitasking and playing multiple roles, you may wonder where is the time to even consider finding yourself. An appealing idea, but one that can seem fairly unachievable. This notion of doing anything for yourself can become a distant reality if you don't put in any effort. All you need is to immerse yourself in this world of media, apps, gadgets and gizmos and your time just flies by.

Since most of your available time is consumed by the digital mediums you engage with, it leaves you with no time at all. The feeling it leads to is a sense of being in a constant rush. Where the time flies by is a question that remains unanswered and the number of hours available in the day become absolutely insufficient to do all that you need to. You may feel the pressure and perpetually experience the feeling of not doing enough, not managing your time well and losing out on doing the things you like and spending time with those you would like to.

Finding that calm space and feeling centred are critical to feel satisfied and content at the end of a busy day. Research has consistently shown that taking breaks from digital media and indulging in other activities instead can help you feel calmer. It may sound paradoxical because when you feel stressed, you automatically reach out for some gadget. Little do you think or realize that this very action is contributing to the stress you may be feeling through the day.

Whether you pick up a gadget to do something related to work—answer a call, respond to a text or mail or just to browse some platform: news, a show or your social media feeds—you inadvertently contribute to the amount of clutter that exists in your mind. None of these actions allows you to be in the moment, absorb it and respond to what is actually going on around you. Instead, you become an extension of what you are reading or seeing on your gadget.

This can border on an unhealthy approach when it becomes a constantly existing reality. It is necessary to be able to take breaks from this approach to see how you are managing yourself and your time.

Disconnect to Connect

Disconnecting is a conscious choice that you must make. Taking steps to ensure your health and well-being requires that you understand the need to disconnect. In order to make connections and to get out of this space where you can experience overwhelming loneliness, you must make efforts to consciously step away from media that can be all-consuming. It can exert a power and control over your actions in an insidious manner, till it reaches a point where you are completely trapped. You need to seek your daily dose of media interaction to feel like the day is complete.

This need to stay connected can become a substantial problem and, as you seek to make connections with people in your day-to-day interactions, you must make efforts to actually engage with them. Getting distracted on account of the technology you are surrounded by is unhelpful. The way you would monitor a child, be firm with them and set boundaries in place about the permissible levels of usage of gadgets, you should consider the same for yourself.

Placing some boundaries around your own actions allows you to take control and feel in charge of the situation. The feeling that others are pushing you to keep your gadget away or stop living through your interactions on social media platforms can make you irritated and unhappy. In its place, making your own choice to prioritize yourself and give yourself the breaks you need, so you can engage with those who surround you, is pleasurable and can make you feel energized and happy.

Being Busy Isn't Glamorous

Society passes along many images of what are presumed to be desirable ways of being and living a life. Being busy has come into this frame as well, in more recent times. Standing out is not easy. Being alone in how you think you must do things can be difficult. Conforming to what is expected in terms of the life you are leading, and the manner in which you are managing yourself, is considered appropriate. Standing out is not necessarily seen in the most positive light. And in all, being busy is getting connoted as the 'in thing'. It is glamorous to be busy and not being so can make you feel like you are a square peg in a round hole.

So you find ways and measures to ensure that you stay busy. Whatever those things may be, from the mundane to the real necessities, everything comes to occupy a big space in your own thoughts and also your conversations with others. You give the impression that there is literally no time that is available to you. You can come across as being non-accommodating, but then you would rather be that than be perceived as being free all the time.

As you spend a substantial amount of time on your gadgets, you must remind yourself that being busy and spending large chunks of time on your gadgets is not useful. Being constantly connected to this virtual world is, instead, disconnecting you from the real world you inhabit.

Is It Really an Emergency?

If you look at your work, you may justify being on your phone continually, or checking for calls, messages and mails by saying that you can't afford to miss anything. You attempt to create this impression in everyone around you that everything reaching you over digital media is critical to what you do. Any missing piece of information can lead to problems of catastrophic proportions.

The question you perhaps need to ask yourself at this point is, 'Is it really an emergency? Would things really collapse if I didn't see or respond to this item?' The answer might actually surprise you. It is likely that a majority of the things that come your way can be allowed to slide for a little while. You can take that break for a few minutes or hours or sometimes even a few days. The world does not come crashing down and work never stops.

You need to find ways to be able to trust the systems you have constructed to deliver at the times you choose to step back or even step away for a bit. The true test of your leadership skills comes in such moments when you let those you lead—be it at work or at home—take on things in their own way, reach their own successes and failures and find their own solutions. Concurrently, you must remember that if there really is an emergency, someone who needs to find you will certainly find a viable mechanism to do so.

Are You Asking Yourself 'Why'?

The key question you need to ask yourself, each time you pull out a gadget or each time you consider pulling out a gadget when you are in a social setting is, 'Why am I doing this now?' If the answer you get is, 'Just like that. It's almost like a habit. I didn't even give it a second thought,' then you must begin to reconsider the approach you have been taking all along.

You need to be able to push yourself to whisk out your gadget only at times when it's really needed. As you try to relax on your own while you're pursuing a cherished hobby or with family or friends, you need to remind yourself from mindlessly pulling out your phone or browsing through an app. It is crucial to remind yourself to be present in the moment.

This anxiety you feel when you are in a social setting which prompts you to immediately reach for your phone makes your gadget feel like a security blanket. You can hide behind it and not have to engage with anybody. You can choose to distance yourself from what is going on around you so that you don't feel any discomfort. This makes you do the very act that you perhaps want to step away from, to ensure you don't keep missing out on forging bonds and making and maintaining your relationships.

Some Things to Consider

Here are some things you can consider as elements which can enable you to indulge in a digital detox. You can find your own pace and maintain a frequency that works for you. But trying out some of these suggested methodologies would certainly help you find the space to be relaxed and focus on the relationships you need in order to combat the loneliness that you experience.

- Set goals that are realistic and not too stringent so that you can ensure you follow a path to reach them. You can keep altering them as you successively accomplish them.
- Remove the excessive alarms and notifications from your gadgets to stop yourself from automatically reaching out for them.
- Take a moment to ask yourself, 'Do I really want to do this?' and then act on the basis of the answer you receive.
- Integrate activities and hobbies into your routine and, while pursuing these, make sure you put your gadgets aside.

- Set boundaries on when and where else you won't use your gadgets, for instance, at the dining table or when you are in a conversation with someone or when you go to use the bathroom or as you get in your car to drive.
- Consider a digital detox which can involve getting off all apps for a few hours or days or switching off a gadget for a duration of time that can work for you.

Slow and Steady Wins the Race

The key to achieving and accomplishing a successful manner of doing a digital detox lies in building it up slowly. You may feel tempted to set lofty targets, especially if you have others around you who are doing the same. Don't let yourself be derailed by everyone else's journey. Instead, find your own pace and work in a comfortable manner to ensure that you take steps which successively lead you to the goals you have set for yourself. You need to be your own monitor and remain committed to yourself to ensure better health, wellness, relationships and quality of life.

21

FOCUS ON LIFESTYLE

A lifestyle change begins with a vision and a single step.

—Jeff Galloway

You can't go back and change the beginning, but you can start where you are and change the ending.

—C.S. Lewis

My mission in life is not merely to survive, but to thrive; and to do so with some passion, some compassion, some humour and some style.

—Maya Angelou

You wake up in the early hours of the morning, wanting to laze around. Before you realize it, lots of time has gone by and you are suddenly late for work. You rush around in a complete frenzy, gathering all your things, throwing together your attire for the day, thinking you're forgetting something but having to run to your car as your bags keep flapping against you. You sit in your car, take a breath and remember that you forgot your laptop. Resigned, you let out a huge sigh, wanting to scream. This is not like your average day but many days do turn out to be like this. But it certainly reminds you of the many days when you had to run and do things, barely having the time for the things you need for a good, healthy lifestyle.

A Less Stressful Life

When you consider lifestyle, it is easy to presume that it indicates the image you reflect to the outside world of the life you are living. From the clothes you wear, the parties you attend, the people you associate with, the amount you travel, the work you do, the money you earn—they are easily assumed to be the fundamentals of the lifestyle you have. Working towards these very elements keep contributing to the stress you experience in your daily living.

It affects your moods. You can feel low or irritable. Worries plague your mind. Anxiety becomes a predominant mechanism through which you respond to many situations around you. You keep craving for a good fix. You may not be a stranger to thoughts like, 'I wish I could just disappear,' 'There must be some way to just close all this,' 'I can't continue to work and live like this,' and, 'I really do need a break'.

There needs to be in place a mechanism that can relieve you of this stressful way of living your life. The whole raison d'être of going through these cycles of industrialization and urbanization and continually striving to uphold your values in the pursuit of your goals has been to have a good life. And if you do a survey, most people will say that a good life means having a relaxed life. Having the means to have a relaxed life is important and you may place different value to how much needs to be done to achieve it. But at the end of the day, each and every person wants to find that tricky balance which allows them to achieve and do well, feel accomplished and yet be able to put their feet up on the couch and just be.

Working towards this state necessitates a strong focus on your lifestyle. It isn't possible that stress would completely dissipate. It has its value in ensuring there is adequate challenge in your life which helps you grow and reach the depths of your potential. But bringing it into a space where it has its positive effect on your life and does not become a debilitating experience, impeding your happiness, thwarting your goals or affecting your health, is imperative.

Follow One Thing at a Time

It is easy to overstretch yourself and have your fingers dipped in too many bowls at the same time. In working to achieve your goals, you don't want to be left behind or feel like you are refusing things which others may have done. This expectation and positive value that has been placed on being a multitasker has led to a false belief that doing multiple things is one of the better abilities to possess. The flip side of being someone who multitasks is that you may not pay adequate attention to critical information and shift your focus of things too soon, before you have been able to complete them to an adequate level.

It is, instead, important to follow the rule of doing and

indulging in one thing at a time. Try to focus on what is there in front of you and attempt to work on that. By reducing the distractions and not allowing yourself to keep getting drawn in different directions, you allow yourself the space to be able to finish things and not feel the stress of not having anything done.

It may feel like there is a chance you may then miss something important. But you don't need to work in absolutes. Maintaining the mental agility and flexibility to be able to recognize when you do need to shift your focus in a situation is important while, by and large, you attempt to maintain a strategy of doing one thing at a time.

Don't Complicate Your Schedule

We call this part having a provision for some contingency planning. If you pack your day and try to force yourself into having a very rigidly structured schedule, you take away from the option of extending the time you may need to do a task or even having to incorporate a new task into the existing schedule you have.

Additionally, this approach will enable you to find time for the breaks you are certainly going to need in your day. No individual can work and function optimally for many hours at a stretch. Everyone needs to include short breaks even as they are working on something. This could mean taking a break to have a glass of water, to use the restroom or to quickly exchange notes with a colleague. It gives you the mental break you need to keep your brain functioning optimally.

Also, it is important not to schedule all the things that are critical on the same day. It would be a very depleting experience cognitively and emotionally if you have to keep firefighting through the day on a regular basis. It helps to space things and ensure that you get a breather in the middle of the important conversations and tasks you have lined up.

Integrate Healthy Habits

The mind and body are connected. If you don't feel good physically, you are likely to experience emotional and psychological distress as well. You should consider focusing on building some healthy habits that work for you and integrate them into your schedules in a comfortable and convenient manner. It is essential that you start slowly and build up the extent to which you are integrating these into your routines so that it does not feel like a very jarring experience and too disruptive to your life.

Simple things can go a long way. A habit of getting in some exercise, some days if not all, is necessary. Given the sedentary lives that most people lead, outdoor activities have become restricted. So find the time to integrate some exercise in a manner that is convenient for you without feeling pressurized to do things that others around you may be doing. Find what works for you and ensure you do allow yourself the time to indulge in it.

Concurrently, focus on your diet and stay away from substances. Despite how tempting things may seem, it is important to ensure that you keep reminding yourself to be mindful of your health.

Inculcate a Habit of Switching Off

Switching off is an important mechanism that is much needed in today's increasingly intrusive world. This switching off is needed not just in terms of the gadgets you use but also from everything that you did in the day. The continuous story that gets played out in your mind of everything that you did, could have done or needs to be done, does not allow you to switch off and keeps your mind overactive in a space that disallows any form of mental relaxation.

So it is imperative to find an activity that allows you to get that mental break. For many, it can come from the music they listen to, others may use exercise as a medium and for others, reading can provide that break from everything. Finding what is helpful for you is a big step forward and, ensuring that you attempt to use it to provide yourself that mental break on a daily basis, is the next important step.

It will be easy to fall out of these habits. But the thing with habits is that they can be restarted and, the more you follow them, the more they get reinforced into your routine.

Wants and Needs Aren't the Same

It is easy to confuse your wants with your needs and keep feeling stress and pressure to make them happen. You may desire many things. But when you ask yourself the question, 'Do I really need this?' or 'Is having this really important for me?' you suddenly realize that you have been looking at certain goals in a manner that causes you more stress.

Relieving this stress and pressure means backing off from

everything that you see as a need and determining whether it really is one or not. You may still want to pursue it despite the clarification you receive in your mind but it would allow you to relieve the pressure and expectation you have built up within your mind. It's also possible that you may recognize that you have probably been somewhat short-sighted in prioritizing things that really do not need your attention as such and that you need to shift focus to other elements.

Be in the Moment

Strive to be in the moment. The past is gone and the future will be what it will be. The only space where you can have any measure of control or effect any change is the present. Focusing on this is empowering. It doesn't let you feel as out of control as you would feel if you were to stay focused on the past or the future. Striving to shift your vantage point and pushing yourself to keep circuiting back to the present is needed so that you can stay focused on making changes in your life and lifestyle today.

Section III

Mindful Urban Living

mindful: Bearing in mind
              Inclined to be aware

When you live in the city, surrounded by all the noise, scuttling about to keep doing everything, you can lose track of your surroundings. Even as city life is enticing and there are always numerous things you can do, you may still find that, over time, your sense of peace and balance can begin to waver. Stress can easily become a predominant feature of your mental state. And you may feel like you are beginning to dread doing some of the daily mundane things that relate to your day-to-day life. Be it running errands, going to the market, meeting with friends, navigating through the traffic—everything induces resistance within you.

You may desperately want to experience a calm state within you and try really hard to manage the enormous number of things that you have to do. Creating the ideal atmosphere at home or around you that allows you to be aware and mindfully engaged with your surroundings and the activities you do can be difficult. What we need in our current environment is a way to be mindfully aware and engaged. Going through each day of life without fully being attuned to how you are living and where you are living can leave you with a strong level of discontent. Days can seem to simply slide by and, before you know it, you have moved through weeks and months and reached the new year as well, without really feeling that you lived through and savoured each day and everything you did.

Even when you try to look back, you may find that your memories are rather blurry. The details are not vividly discernible and everything is just a bullet point in the list of things you did do. How you felt at those times, what you thought, how you negotiated your way or made decisions, have simply vanished. The factual details are all present and life is just slipping away slowly but steadily.

Being aware is not just being informed and attuned to what is happening around you. You need to be in the moment. Experience it, even if you don't enjoy it. Whether it leads to the experience of negative emotions or difficult situations, it is essential to stay connected. Concurrently, all of this must happen as you push yourself to refrain from judgments which make the task a little difficult. Being in the right space emotionally and mentally is crucial.

It is all well to talk of yoga and meditation retreats. But it doesn't serve any purpose if you cannot integrate these practices into your daily living. Simply utilizing a few days in the year or an hour a day when you give yourself the time to focus on you and your mental, emotional and psychological well-being is not going to be sufficient because the pressures will keep mounting. Instead, being able to maintain mindfulness in your daily existence can lead to substantial dividends.

Start by De-Cluttering

You begin this process by starting to de-clutter. Your mind, the spaces you occupy and utilize—all would benefit from going through a spring cleaning of sorts. Having mounds of clutter around you can be stress-inducing and impact your health in a detrimental manner.

De-cluttering and organizing have become aspects that are much talked about today. When Marie Kondo, Japanese organizing consultant, author and TV show host, spoke of her KonMari method, little did one know that it would become such a valuable lesson. But when we speak of de-cluttering here, we also want it to move beyond the physical spaces that Kondo was talking about. It needs to become a practice, something that you automatically gravitate towards in every sphere of your life.

De-cluttering the physical space around you—your desk, room, bathroom, kitchen, cupboards, hallway—all contribute to creating a feeling of relaxation. Having lesser things around you, which can seem paradoxical, considering we live in a culture of wanting more and more, actually helps you feel less cluttered even within. You may be nostalgic about many things but their presence may not add value to your life today. In fact, the overwhelming quantities of objects will only create overwhelming thoughts in your mind, not allowing you to feel relaxed.

You would find it surprising that this simple act of purging things from your surroundings can, in itself, lead to clearing up of spaces even within your mind. Research consistently shows that de-cluttering energizes you, reduces anxiety, makes you feel confident and also boosts your self-esteem.

Know Your Body

To be mindfully attuned to yourself you need to be aware of what goes on within your body. The stress that gets created within it and the tension that occurs when you face specific situations, can all guide you towards determining ways of being able to manage yourself in a good way. In most scenarios, we end up pushing ourselves a lot. We keep disregarding the signals that our body sends us and keep trying to stretch ourselves a little more each time, to be able to satisfy those insatiable demands that keep getting placed upon us all the time.

In order to live a good life, it then becomes imperative that you become more consciously aware of what goes on with your body. Taking care of your body is important and responding to its needs is vital. Ignoring the signs that it gives you can be a strategy that works in the short run in case of exigent circumstances. But this is not an approach that would give you dividends in the long run.

In order to become more deeply attuned to your body you can consider practising deep breathing and relaxation exercises. Using different exercises to connect with and understand the needs of your body is helpful in ensuring your overall health and well-being. You can turn to specific meditative practices for the same as well.

In being aware of your body and its needs, you also learn to be gentle with it. You give yourself the opportunity to understand it and grow. This compassion you demonstrate to yourself by being more mindfully attuned to your physical body can also come to embody the approach you adopt towards others around you, becoming more gentle and kind in your interactions with them as well.

Understand Your Fears

Being mindfully attuned to yourself involves understanding your fears. Understand that most of your fears have emanated from the interactions you have had with your environment and within the context of your relationships. Your mind derived associations, created assumptions and started viewing things in certain ways that kept the fears in place.

Everyone wishes that bad things won't come their way. Some may even believe that all the bad things they see others struggling to cope with can never be a reality of their existence. Or, people may be stuck with thoughts of how they will handle bad situations and manage negative outcomes when they or their loved ones happen to be in such spaces. It can be scary to think of having to deal with so much yourself. Finding that courage can be difficult to imagine. And, so, you may want to run away from these thoughts and imaginings.

In attempting to disconnect from your fears, worries and anxieties, you would get increasingly distant from your own inner self. The mindful approach that is needed in order to effectively respond to the situations of your life would then go missing in this scenario. So, to integrate mindfulness into your daily living, you need to be willing to face and understand your fears.

Allowing those difficult thoughts to come into your mind is needed because intertwined with fear is also the capacity to be fearless. In allowing yourself to experience vulnerability you also create the opportunity to grow through experiences. It remains important to remember to be gentle with yourself and not engage in passing stringent judgments.

Allowing your fears to be there and not being driven to run away or towards them, letting them and yourself be, while continually responding to what is going on around you, is an approach that you would need to embrace in being attuned to yourself and your life.

Know What You Put in

There is much that your mind infers and processes across situations. A lot of this can happen in a fairly unconscious manner. Striving to stay aware of what is reaching your mind from your environment, the importance you are giving it and the meaning you are attributing to it, is required to ensure you feel calm and have control over what goes on with you.

Just like it is advocated that you should be aware of the food you consume and not shovel things in mindlessly, without assessing if you're really hungry and whether your body really needs it, it is advocated that you need to find a similar strategy for what you put into your mind. Asking yourself simple questions like, 'Do I really need to expend energy and effort into thinking about this?' 'Is it going to be helpful to engage in such a deep analysis of this?' 'Should

I simply refrain from getting myself entangled in this?' or 'Do I really need to fix it?' can help you reassess the way you direct your thought process as well as your actions.

Concurrently, the information and media you consume dictates the amount of clutter that gets accumulated within you. Mindlessly watching and absorbing all the content that reaches you is not helpful. In its place, it is crucial to determine what you really enjoy and what contributes to your growth, and filter out all the other things that only contribute to increasing the clutter within you. Besides this, constantly and continually being on different social media platforms and using gadgets all the time can be detrimental to your health and also take away from the time you spend in nurturing your relationships.

Living Lightly

Our days can be intense and the way we think and feel about them can also be equally so. A very important aspect of living mindfully is not getting stuck and wrapped up in this constant tug of war that occurs in your thoughts and emotions. It is important to reinforce the need to exist lightly within what your mind creates and the emotional experiences you have.

What would aid you to live lightly is learning to laugh whether you are confronted by the good or the bad and taking things lightly by attempting to refrain from attaching too much meaning, excessive judgment and excess value to them. Humour is, in fact, a healthy defence mechanism to have in your armour. Psychology has reiterated the important role humour can play in diffusing situations and allowing you to reduce the intensity of the emotion you may be feeling. It will certainly not be an effective strategy to apply across all situations but applying it prudently would be helpful.

In attempting to live within the present moment, as is advocated by mindfulness practices, you need to be overly zealous in disallowing your thoughts from wandering. Creativity happens in the spaces where you are able to let yourself be and float lightly. Permit yourself to indulge in some of this as well and be gentle and self-compassionate when you do encourage yourself to keep engaging with the present moment.

The Small Spaces for Mindful Living

There are numerous smaller moments in our lives where you can integrate the practices of a mindful living. Keep these in your conscious awareness to build within yourself contentment and happiness:

1. During your morning routines and rituals
2. When you go for your walk
3. As you sip your cup of tea or coffee
4. When you consume your meals
5. In your conversations with people
6. As you travel from one destination to another
7. When you listen to music during the day
8. As you engage in cooking for yourself or your family
9. When you sit down to watch a show
10. As you text someone or call them over the phone

You would be going through a number of these situations

on a daily basis. Take the time to remind yourself in these moments to be fully present. Engage with the action more fully and immerse yourself in it. Try not to get distracted too often. It will take you time to find the momentum, but if you keep persisting, you will discover the ability to be mindfully present and engaged to your life in this urban jungle that you occupy.

A Final Word

Take things slow. The fast-paced nature of everything is what contributes to the feeling of disengagement and disconnect. Make a concerted effort to slow down the pace at which you are moving. Find the energy to remind yourself about the need to just take the time to do things slowly. Ask yourself, 'Do I really need to be in this rush?' More often than not, the answer will be 'no'. Stop looking at how others around you are operating. Make this choice for yourself and find the pace that works best for you. By moving slowly, you will observe more and absorb more and that will help you be more mindfully connected to your world.

Section IV

Section IV

Adapting to Change: Learning from the Pandemic

adapt: To make fit (as for a new use) often by modification

The COVID-19 pandemic brought to the fore many challenges for the entire population. Even as you would have been working towards building a life and engaging in self-care, attempting to beat the day-to-day loneliness of urban existence, the pandemic threw a spanner in all those attempts, pushing you to face an even graver reality. What the pandemic did was push you to recognize what true loneliness can be and how unprepared you are to cope with it. You assumed, like most others around you, that it would not, in fact could not, last for too long. The thought was that this whole situation would soon wear off and life would be back to 'normal'. Despite the challenges of that past normal, it was still a better one and one that you had developed mechanisms to accommodate, adjust and cope with.

The last year and a half have borne testimony to diverse issues, which you might have had to face, without the presence of true support systems. Many have experienced difficulties for lack of significant relationships—personally and at workplaces. Others felt the loss of their livelihoods or the stress of potentially losing their livelihoods. Many went through substantial loss and had to grieve the sudden loss of their friends and family members—those who were perfectly healthy and hale and hearty too collapsed in the face of the infection this virus brought. There was intense fear that you could feel and that was compounded by the complete uncertainty of how and when things would change.

The indefiniteness and ambiguity of the whole situation has perplexed all. It has created intense anxiousness and worry in the minds of many. Negative thought patterns have found their way into your mind perhaps. There is apprehension and trepidation around how things will likely unfold. Many experienced dips in their moods, questioning their relationships, the choices they have made, the lives they have led, perhaps even their very existence and what kind of world we are creating and leaving for generations to come. Existential concerns have been on a rise as has a preoccupation with how we can maintain safety.

Meanwhile, there have also been those who have taken a rather callous approach to the whole situation and that too has, in itself, led to many perturbations in the minds of those around them. There has been a questioning of the ways in which human beings look at the welfare of larger groups and segments of the population. And these questions have emphasized the need to focus on building the altruistic and prosocial spirit of the population so that we can come together collectively to support each other in such tough times.

We have learnt many things during this past year and here are some of the essentials that must be a focal concern for all.

Support Systems Are Critical

The value of building support systems has always been of critical importance. This pandemic has led to an upsurge in the need to focus on building and sustaining these even more. Whether you live alone or in a family system, creating and maintaining relationships that provide you with the required emotional and psychological nourishment is important. Having people who you can rely on and turn to in case you struggle is required. No other time period has emphasized this more to us than this pandemic.

Whether young or old, everyone has found a way of adapting to the challenges posed by not being able to physically meet with people. Virtual platforms became a lifeline and allowed you to connect with even those you had been disconnected from for many years. Relationships you would not have approached previously too were refurbished during this period. You would have connected with neighbours and other community dwellers who you might not have ever known previously.

We now recognize the need to focus not just on those few essential friendships and familial relationships but also build our community connect. Make that extra effort to know those who live around you. Step out and reach out to them too because these are the immediate support systems who would be able to connect and provide you with the much-needed support during critical times.

Move One Step at a Time

Too often we want to know what life will be a few years down the line and, when that predictability is missing, it rattles us and scares us. We struggle to cope with a situation that we feel we might not be privy to in advance. A big learning that has emerged during this pandemic is the need to move one step at a time. More often than not, we can be faced with circumstances and life situations that will not be predictable. It highlights the need to be flexible in allowing yourself to look at what is there in front of you and make the choice that is most logical, pragmatic and appealing in that given circumstance.

This is an approach that might not have been the first option for most. However, we now do recognize that focusing on what is there in front of you, and making choices that provide the best approach in that given circumstance, is the best way forward. It is critical that you constantly give yourself reminders to stay calm and collected even though you cannot foresee the distant future. Stay committed towards making choices with the information you do have and maintain your trust and belief in yourself, and the support systems you have cultivated, to be able to manage the contingencies that can and will arise in time.

Be Kind to Yourself

In all that you would have experienced, you may have realized that we have a tendency to be harsh and overly critical of our own selves and our actions. There is a strong need to learn to be kind to your own self. Being compassionate towards the experiences you have been having is important as is the need to not become overly judgmental of the choices you are making. Give yourself the space to make mistakes as to err in the face of challenging situations is a normal experience.

It is also critical that you embrace your own experiences. You would be going through a plethora of emotions and, often, even those around you might struggle to understand what is happening. Keep sharing but also keep embracing what you are experiencing. Whether it is anxiety or low moods or a sense of dissonance and disconnection or a feeling that leads you to question things and relationships around you, you need to let yourself go through these emotional experiences and then work towards resolving the dilemmas and dichotomies that you face.

Be Proactive in Resolving Conflicts

We often adopt an approach where we let things be. It is easy to allow problems to stew and keep manifesting in different forms and formats, especially when we stay immersed in our day-to-day lives. There are innumerable distractions that can allow the continuing utilization of such an approach, where you can steer clear of the problems and not do much to resolve them. Other things can instead come into play and occupy your attention.

In the pandemic, you perhaps did not get a chance to disconnect from the problematic experiences. Being stuck in spaces and with people from which the previously available distractions could not provide respite pushed you to consider an alternative approach. What has gotten highlighted during this period is the need to be proactive in working through problems and conflicts. Instead of allowing things to just be and not taking an approach that is oriented towards resolution, it is critical that you look towards resolving conflicts. A problem-solving approach allows you to feel in greater control and also enhances the quality of the relationships you have around you.

Emotional experiences should not be negated and you must acknowledge and accept what you are going through. But concurrently work towards seeking a way to pull yourself and your relationships out of the zone of conflict and aversion so your support systems can be more effective.

Build Individual Skills

Over the years, fun and joy have gotten associated with going out and being with others. Surrounding yourself with people has been an approach that has become the unwinding routine for a large percentage of the population. You might have even forgotten effective ways to spend time with your own self. Having too much time on your hands is typically utilized in navigating through various over-the-top (OTT) platforms and consuming more content on social media platforms.

It is critical that you adopt a more holistic approach where, besides spending extensive time with friends and family, you also make a proactive effort to build on your own individual areas of interest and hone your personal skill sets. Being able to do things on your own and harness your interests and hobbies has never been more important. It is crucial that you make a proactive effort in doing so and adopt an approach where you can take care of, and spend good quality time, with yourself.

Be Responsible

It is critical that, in order to take care of yourself, your relationships and to feel and maintain the effectiveness of your approach in doing all that you do, you also work towards being responsible. This responsibility is towards yourself, your family and the community and also in how you are in your online spaces. Looking towards others to be your support system is not possible unless you also make a proactive effort to be responsible otherwise.

Take care of your roles at home and at work. Ensure you uphold the norms that are put in place to maintain safety and security of all. Be a responsible social media consumer. Don't troll others or engage in cyber bullying. Be an upstander and take an approach where you make the right choices. This too would go a long way in buttressing your social support systems, enabling you to tackle the loneliness we have all experienced in multiple ways during this pandemic.

A Final Word

Focus on the collective good. More than anything else, what has come across very strongly during this period is the need to work towards becoming a society that is supportive of all its members. This pandemic has highlighted that we all need to come together in difficult times and find ways to support each other. The collective good is what would lead to the best outcomes, always. It is important that while making the choices, we think not just about what makes us happy but also about what is good for those around us—our near and dear ones.

This approach of focusing on the collective good is something that would help ensure that, in the long run, we create a society that inculcates and teaches the right values and ethics to the young population and future generations.